The Land They Left Behind

Canada's Ukrainians in the Homeland

Hutsuls selling a cow at the market in Kosiu

The Land They Left Behind

Canada's Ukrainians in the Homeland

by Stella Hryniuk and Jeffrey Picknicki   Introduction by Nadia Valášková   Photography by František Řehoř

WATSON DWYER
PUBLISHING LIMITED

Dedicated to the memory of František Řehoř

Designed by Doowah Design Inc.

Photographs reproduced with the kind permission of Sisters Servants of Mary Immaculate, Canadian Province Administration Centre, 5 Austin Terrace, Toronto, ON M5R 1Y1.

Published with the assistance of the Manitoba Arts Council and The Canada Council.

Printed in Canada by Hignell Printing Ltd.

Canadian Cataloguing in Publication Data

Hryniuk, Stella M., 1939-

    The Land They Left Behind

    Includes bibliographical references and index
    ISBN 0-920486-13-4

1. Peasantry -Ukraine, Western - History - Pictorial works.

2. Ukraine, Western - History - Pictorial works.

I. Hryniuk, Stella M., 1939-　II. Řehoř, František　III. Title

DK508.9.U37H79 1995   947'.718082'0222 C95-920169-6

TABLE OF CONTENTS

PREFACE

This book was conceived back in 1989 and has taken a number of years and a lot of important people to come into being.

I first became aware of František Řehoř and his legacy through a colleague, P.R. Magocsi, Chair of Ukrainian Studies in Toronto. He was in contact with Mykola Mušinka in Prague whose wife's sister, Nadia Valášková, a professional ethnographer, had discovered in the course of her work this valuable photo collection in the National Museum of Ethnography in the Czech capital. She had become interested in Řehoř and delved into his collected works, writing articles, delivering scholarly papers about him, and promoting a wider interest in him. In 1990, she began corresponding with me. She was imbued with admiration for Řehoř, and fervently hoped that his work could become better known in Canada and elsewhere. Through her efforts and enthusiasm, I was able to get to see the full collection of Řehoř's pictures for the first time in Canada in 1992. But to be able to publish or exhibit them, the Prague Museum required payment for purchase of the copyright. It was another woman, Sister Ambrose Stachiw, Provincial Superior for the Canadian province of the Sisters Servants of Mary Immaculate, who made this possible. She arranged to have her community buy the photos and to permit me to publish and exhibit them.

Once I had them in hand, the need arose to create an explanatory text, to convey to the reader the significance of the activities portrayed in the photos. Jeffrey Picknicki, a recent MA graduate from the University of Manitoba's Department of Slavic Studies, took on this task with whole-hearted dedication and stamina. The text, except for Chapter One, is his achievement in which I played a role of historical consultant and editor in shaping the final product.

What is remarkable about the pictures and what so attracted me and all those along the way to publication was the truthful and careful exposition of what is now a vanished world. They faithfully depict the warmth and strength of the awakening village of Eastern Galicia, with its Ukrainian, Jewish and Polish and other population. Clearly František Řehoř was captivated by this world, and probably sensed that it was disappearing. The photos confirm what I and a few others have found when we studied this society in depth. The village life of the late 19th century in Eastern Galicia was not one of grinding poverty. It was rather a life centred around an efficient, self-reliant, cooperative style of agriculture, conducted by people who loved their land, and were deeply attached to their traditions and religious faith. It was this which sustained those of them who came to Canada as immigrants to a much harsher climate and landscape.

Over the last six years, working with all of the people concerned to have this book produced has been a learning experience for me. I have relied heavily on the research and writing talents of Jeffrey Picknicki. Throughout, what has been the motivating factor is the idea that these photos of East European villagers at work and play would be made available for more people to see.

I am grateful for the grant awarded me by the T. Shevchenko Foundation to assist in the preparation of this book.

STELLA HRYNIUK, JULY 1995

I remember exactly when this book began for me. I saw the photographs for the first time in 1990 and was immediately and completely captivated by these images. Sitting at Stella's kitchen table and looking at the sights, the scenes, the faces—it was a collection the likes of which I had never seen before and one whose story, as I would later find out, had waited over a century to be told. Months of research, here in Canada and in Europe, translation of source materials in three languages and writing produced the text which you have before you. The work was, as trite as it sounds, truly a labour of love.

My participation on this project provided me the pleasure of meeting and working with Dr. Nadia Valášková, a researcher at the Institute of Ethnology of the Czech Academy of Sciences in Prague, who from its inception has played a vital role in the preparation of this volume. Since our first meeting in 1990 she assisted me immeasurably in obtaining various source materials, acted as a consultant on the writing of the text and during a visit to Prague in 1994 enabled me to examine materials from Řehoř's files at the Literary Archive, see a sample of the artifacts from his ethnographic collection at the National Museum and, to complete the pilgrimage, visit his grave in the city's Olšany cemetery. Without her help, guidance and contributions my work would have been considerably more difficult and the end result clearly diminished. For this I am eternally grateful.

I also wish to express my gratitude to Maria Valo and Petro Babiak of the Naukova biblioteka im. V. Stefanyka and to Myroslava Diadiuk and Tania Semeniv of the Tsentralnyi derzhavnyi istorychnyi arkhiv in Lviv for their assistance during my work on Řehoř and the photograph collection in Ukraine and in forwarding additional materials to Canada. Nevenka Koscevic and Vladimira Zvonik of the Slavic Collection, Elizabeth Dafoe Library, University of Manitoba, provided me with further valuable information and materials, especially in researching village names and locations.

A few words must be said also about the text. In its conceptualization and preparation, a conscious effort was made throughout to keep as its base the rich material and spiritual folk culture of the Ukrainians of East Galicia. In this regard I have drawn extensively on the best available ethnographic sources relevant to the place and the period, especially those by Kolberg, Moszyński and Shukhevych, and many of Řehoř's own articles, unpublished writings and research notes. For the rendering of Ukrainian words into English I have used the Modified Library of Congress System of Cyrillic Transliteration with the following variants: я-ya, ю-yu, є-ye, ï-yi and й-y when occuring initially. As a convenience for the reader, a glossary of Ukrainian words is also provided. Czech words appear in their original forms and, where necessary, with English translations. All dates within the text are given according to the Julian calendar (also referred to as "Old Style") which was used by the Ukrainians in East Galicia at that time. From March 1, 1800 there was a 12-day difference between the Julian and Gregorian calendars and a 13-day difference from March 1, 1900.

František Řehoř, through his tireless work and selfless dedication to the Ukrainians of Galicia, has left us a wonderful legacy. His photographs, writings and collections speak volumes about the cultural heritage that we as Ukrainians share and of which we can be proud. A people which he embraced as his own still claims him as one its heroes and it is to his memory and with deepest admiration that this book is dedicated.

JEFFREY PICKNICKI, JULY 1995

The Life and Work of the Photographer, František Řehoř

by Nadia Valášková   (Translated by Jeffrey Picknicki)

František Řehoř. His long list of accomplishments belies his relatively short life of 42 years. He was an ethnographer, folklorist, collector, writer and, as will be revealed in the pages of this volume, photographer of a spectacular collection of images being published herein for the first time since they were taken over 100 years ago. By birth he was a Czech but he lived for much of his life in Ukrainian Galicia, a region whose unique ethnic colouring and rich culture so fascinated the young Řehoř that he dedicated the whole of his creative life and work to its study and documentation.

Řehoř's legacy, in addition to his photograph collection, is both large and varied. As an ethnographer and folklorist, he amassed through his field work and research a wealth of written material on a myriad of topics dealing with Ukrainian folk and material culture. His East Galician ethnographic collection, presently housed at the National Museum in Prague, consists of approximately 2,000 different items of Ukrainian folk art and craft. His library, with an inventory of several thousand volumes, was donated to the Ukrainian library at the Czech Royal Museum (today the National Museum in Prague) and the library of the Prosvita Society in Lviv, Ukraine. To his credit as a writer go approximately 300 articles and encyclopedia entries on Ukrainian themes which were first published in the Czech press and then in the scholarly dictionary *Ottův slovník naučný*, his diaries and journals and his personal correspondence from nearly 200 individuals, many prominent figures from Czech and Ukrainian cultural and community life of that time. It is no exaggeration that this dedicated and hard-working Czech, although he died before realizing all of his plans in the field of Ukrainian studies, made a significant and valuable contribution to the study of Ukrainian, specifically East Galician, culture.

František Řehoř (pronounced, approximately in English, Frántishek Rzhéhorzh) was born in eastern Bohemia in the village of Stěžery, near Hradec Králové, on December 16, 1857, the second of five children born to Josef and Františka Řehoř. He completed his secondary schooling in Hradec Králové and while still a student displayed a keen interest in literature, history and the collection of artifacts relating to the natural sciences. He also had a talent and inclination for writing and his diaries contain a great deal of information relating to Czech ethnography. On the basis of stories and reminiscences from his parents and other family members, Řehoř wrote and documented his family history to the end of the seventeenth century.

Introduction

Řehoř's father, in learning about the opportunity of buying or leasing landholdings in East Galicia, travelled there and decided to lease a manor in the village of Vovkiv Hrabynka near Lviv (now Vovkiv, Peremyshliany county). Shortly thereafter, his mother Františka, sisters Anna and Maria (his youngest sister Františka died as a child) and his younger brother Jan also left their native village in Bohemia and joined his father. František himself left for Galicia on July 9, 1877, from which time the village of Vovkiv became his second home for almost 13 years. He worked with his father on the manor but what was most interesting for him was the rich and unusual folk culture of the Ukrainian people among whom he was now living. He would later write:

Even as a child I felt an immediate attachment to the Ukrainians. It was fate which brought me to live among them and to come to know these people. I fell completely in love with the Ukrainians. In good times and in bad, I would gladly bend the heavens for them…

Providing an impulse for his deeper interest in the culture of the Ukrainian people was an article which appeared in the Czech press about the well-known Czech cultural and political activist Vojta Náprstek and his České průmyslové muzeum (Czech Technical Museum) in Prague. This museum and the husband and wife team of Vojta (1826–1894) and Josefa (1838–1907) Náprstek came to play a significant role in the life of František Řehoř and also in Czech-Ukrainian relations at that time. In learning about the museum, Řehoř wrote his first letter to Náprstek in 1878 in which he proposed collecting and sending artifacts from East Galicia to Prague. He responded positively to this proposition, thus marking the beginning of the working relationship and close friendship between Řehoř and the Náprsteks, who were known for their altruism, and who provided him with invaluable help and support.

Řehoř's private life was marked with much unhappiness but his work and travels in East Galicia brought him joy and inner peace. He was deaf and often in ill health but with great enthusiasm delved into his beloved Ukrainian world to work with the materials which he had collected. His mother and older sister Anna died while the family was living in Vovkiv. His brother Jan, ill with tuberculosis, was sent to Moravia for treatment but died shortly thereafter. His father, who left Galicia for the family's native Stěžery, remarried and raised a second family. In 1890, Řehoř himself having taken ill, travelled to Moravia to recover. Respected and admired for his work, he was honoured with a festive gathering prepared by several prominent Ukrainian cultural and community activists in Lviv prior to his departure.

In Moravia, as soon as his health improved, Řehoř began sending Moravian artifacts to the museum in Prague. Then, while living in Stěžery, he worked at systematizing his East Galician ethnographic and folkloric materials and tried to secure for himself employment. He received a small amount of money from his father and published articles on a regular basis but this was not enough on which to live. In 1891, with his sister and brother-in-law now living in the village of Zarohyzno near Zhydachiv, Řehoř returned to East Galicia to live with them and continue his ethnographic fieldwork. He received some financial support for research from the editors of *Svatobor* and the Czech Academy of Sciences, Literature and Art together with the assistance he received from the Náprsteks. He went on research trips and he recorded, illustrated, photographed and collected artifacts which he sent to Prague and undertook further ethnographic work with his correspondents from the ranks of the intelligentsia and clergy. He planned a complex study of the material and spiritual culture of the East Galician Ukrainians and dreamed about publishing his work independently. Unfortunately, this was not to be.

In time, Řehoř's sister and brother-in-law sold the manor in Zarohyzno and in November 1893 he returned to Prague where a friend helped him find a job as an official in the city's Public Library. From time to time he continued to travel to Galicia to do further ethnographic fieldwork and collect materials and lived very modestly in order to save money for further research trips. When he became ill and was unable to work, he was supported by his friends. In Prague, he maintained a vigourous correspondence with his many Galician and Bukovynian colleagues and acquaintances. As an example, Řehoř's files in the Literary Archives of the Památník národního písemnictví in Prague contain 160 letters from Volodymyr Shukhevych who was also involved in the study of Ukrainian ethnography.

In June 1899, Řehoř travelled to Galicia once again. The Ukrainian press reported on his arrival and appealed to the public to assist him in his ethnographic work. The response was overwhelming and numerous artifacts in the museum collection date from this particular year. He was warmly received everywhere he went as a friend, colleague and compatriot of the Ukrainians. When he left Galicia, no one thought that it would be forever. On October 6, 1899, when his friend A. Černý, the editor of the newly founded newspaper *Slovanský přehled*, brought him the latest edition to his flat in Prague, he found František Řehoř dead.

With the news of his death, telegrams with expressions of deepest sympathy were sent to Prague from all over East Galicia. Czech, Ukrainian and other newspapers published announcements of his death, the funeral and other obituary notices. The celebrated Ukrainian writer and poet Ivan Franko wrote that Řehoř's premature death was a tragedy for the Galician Ukrainians. Prominent Czech leaders and activists, his friends and Ukrainians living in Prague were present at the funeral. At the Olšany cemetery in Prague where he was buried, a monument was built in his honour and a memorial plaque was placed in his native village of Stěžery in 1902.

In time, Řehoř and his work came to be forgotten and, like the photographs, much of his materials remained untouched for decades. After World War I, however, when Carpatho-Ukraine became a part of the newly created Czechoslovakia, the Czechs turned increased attention towards Ukrainian studies. Beginning in the 1950s, articles about Řehoř began appearing, first by Míchal Molnár, who organized a commemorative celebration in Stěžery on the occasion of the 55th anniversary of his death, and a small exhibit of his East Galician collection was prepared by the Ethnographic Museum in Prague. In 1990, a symposium in Lviv called "The History of Ukrainian, Czech and Slovak Cultural Ties" was dedicated to Řehoř's memory and in the village of Vovkiv, his home for much of his time in Galicia, an inscribed marble plate was placed in his honour.

Perhaps one of Řehoř's greatest achievements is his photograph collection. Rediscovered only a few years ago, the collection consists of 350 glass plates, 9 x 12 cm in size, and is currently held at the National Museum in Prague. In the 1890s, Řehoř published approximately 70 of the photographs in the Czech press (44 in the journal *Světozor* in 1894 together with an article entitled "A Journey through Galician Rus" which appeared as a series) and a small number also appeared in the Lviv newspaper *Zoria*. The majority of these negatives, however, were not saved by the editors of the newspapers and journals and no longer exist.

The first mentions about Řehoř as a photographer are found in his diaries from 1874–77 in which he writes that he borrowed a camera and did some photographing in Stěžery. It appears that he did not have a camera of his own even during his time in Galicia. Otherwise, his photographic documentation would have been more extensive. The photographs were taken during the period 1891–93 when Řehoř lived in Zarohyzno near Zhydachiv in East Galicia. His accompanying notes provide no precise dates but he did write about his photographic work in his letters. Upon returning from Podillia in May 1892, for example, he wrote to the Náprsteks from Zarohyzno: "Other than the notes, I have also taken several dozen photographs. As an example, I am sending a copy of the Easter game 'zhuchok' performed by Ruthenian girls…" and on October 13, 1892, he wrote: "I was just in Zhydachiv to photograph the weekly market."

Thematically, the photograph collection can be divided into several groups. There are images showing traditional clothing (both festive and everyday), occupations (field work, domestic chores, trade, craft), holidays and rituals (both calendar and family), games, dances and markets. Not all of these groups, however, are equal in size and some, such as christenings, weddings and other family celebrations are completely absent from the collection even though Řehoř himself participated in these events and described them in his articles. The reason, of course, was his lack of a camera of his own and the inability to photograph the interiors of houses or buildings because of technical considerations.

Territorially, the collection includes, first of all, Zhydachiv and its environs and also several villages in the former counties of Stryi, Dolyna, Kalush, Tovmach and Kosiv in the Hutsul region and Horodenka and Ternopil in Podillia (over 30 places in all). This represents only about a quarter of the places which Řehoř visited and from where he collected the ethnographic artifacts for the museum in Prague.

The photographic collection, it cannot be overstated, exists within the legacy of Řehoř's life and work truly as an anomaly. Taken with a borrowed camera and at a time when photography as a part of ethnographic fieldwork was seldom used, the photographs reconstruct in considerable detail the social and cultural ambience of the era as it was seen by someone who lived through it. From the characteristic village architecture to the work in the fields to the joyous Easter celebrations and the bustling atmosphere of the market place, they exist as visual testimony to the rich and vibrant life that was the Galician homeland.

International boundary
Provincial boundary

WESTERN GALICIA

EASTERN GALICIA

Lviv

Ternopil

LEMKO REGION

Zhydachiv

Stryi

Terebovlia

BOIKO REGION

Kalush

Dolyna

KINGDOM OF HUNGARY

Tovmach

Horodenka

HUTSUL REGION

TRANSCARPATHIA

Kosiv

BUKOVYNA

ROMANIA

N

Eastern Galicia

Shaded areas are countries
where the photographs
were taken.

POLAND

WESTERN GALICIA

EASTERN GALICIA

UKRAINE

SLOVENIA

HUNGARY

MOLDAVIA

ROMANIA

YUGOSLAVIA

0   100 km

BULGARIA

Sea of Azov

Black Sea

0   50
kilometres

Produced by The Cartography Office, Department of Geography, University of Toronto

1

The harvest in Tyshkivtsi, Horodenka county

The land where the people in the photographs in this book lived, and from which most of the Ukrainian settlers in Canada prior to 1914 came, was the province of Galicia (Halychyna) in the Austrian Empire. The Ukrainians lived in the eastern portion of this province, East Galicia, most of which is nowadays in Western Ukraine. It was a region with its own history and tradition, but it was hardly ever an independent entity. Instead, it had a number of political masters who imposed their rule and something of their way of life on it, though peasant culture was not fundamentally affected. In the early Middle Ages, East Galicia was the centre of a principality called Halych, and part of the Kievan Rus state. In the fourteenth century it was incorporated into the Polish-Lithuanian Commonwealth. In the sixteenth century it became part of the Polish Commonwealth, which was partitioned in the late 1700s. Galicia (and Bukovyna) then became part of the Habsburg domains—the Habsburgs being the ruling family of Austria—and remained so until the end of World War I in 1918.

In the north and east, East Galicia bordered on the Tsarist Russian Empire, and in the south and south-east on Hungary and Bukovyna, which

During the centuries that East Galicia was ruled by Polish kings, almost all the originally Ukrainian nobility had become "polonized," that is they had adopted a Polish way of life, spoke Polish, had become Roman Catholic, and generally felt themselves to be Poles. Other nobles were descendants of Polish aristocrats who had been granted estates in East Galicia by Poland's kings. As was not unusual in Europe, the nobility owned large estates, often in a number of different locations. The estates or manors of the lesser nobility and gentry were smaller, but often still sizeable. The great majority of the population were peasants. Until 1848 they, Ukrainians and Poles alike, had been compelled to perform compulsory labour for a number of days each week on the nobles' estates, in return for which they were allocated land which they cultivated for themselves. The division of land in 1848 between the noble or gentry landowner and the peasantry disadvantaged the latter, who often possessed only a small area from which to sustain their families. Until the second half of the nineteenth century, Jews had not been allowed to own land. Consequently most of them lived in the many small towns of East Galicia, in which they frequently formed the majority of the population.

The Land of the Photographs CHAPTER 1

were both part of the Habsburg's Austro-Hungarian Monarchy. In the west the river San drew the line between East (predominantly Ukrainian) and West (or Polish) Galicia. East Galicia was a region of several changing landscapes, from the Carpathian mountains in the south, with peaks as high as 2000 meters, to rolling terrain often deeply intersected by rivers and streams, to flatlands vulnerable to flooding. The climate varied with the terrain, from a continental type with cold winters and raw winds in the north-west to rather warmer conditions in the south-east. Much of the land had good black soil on which a variety of crops could be grown; at higher altitudes and also in some other parts there were extensive forests and woodlands, with wild game such as boars and bears.

From the time for which we have historical records onwards, Ukrainians have formed the core population of East Galicia, but as always they lived interspersed with others in the nineteenth century. According to the 1890 census, East Galicia had a population of about 3,850,000. Of these around 64 percent were Ukrainian; about 20 percent were Polish, and about 13.5 percent were Jews. The remainder were mostly German agricultural settlers. The Ukrainians were Greek Catholic by religion, while the Poles were predominantly Roman Catholic.

They were usually artisans and craftsmen, traders, peddlars and shopkeepers. They were shopkeepers in the villages too, as well as innkeepers and estate stewards.

As of the 1890s, when the photographs were taken, 80 percent of East Galicia's people derived their income from agriculture. There was only one large city, Lviv, the capital of Galicia, with a population of almost 110,000. There were a few large towns with between 15,000 and 30,000 people, such as Kolomyia, Peremyshl, Stanyslaviv and Ternopil. There were few large scale industries: some railway workshops and tobacco factories, a large flour-mill, two large lumber and timber operations. There was also a petroleum industry in Drohobych county, as well as many brickworks and small flour and saw mills. The countryside was quite densely populated, except in the mountain areas, and villagers were accustomed to the closeness of their neighbours. The villages themselves were often along the slopes of valleys, in a long ribbon development. Ukrainian and Polish villagers at times lived alongside each other; sometimes, however, a village might have sections that were predominantly Ukrainian or Polish.

Galicia was the largest province, or Crownland, of the Austrian Empire. At the head of the state was the Emperor Francis Joseph, who ruled for 68 years (1848–1916) and who was much revered by most East Galician Ukrainians. Austria was a constitutional monarchy after 1868. A parliament for all of Austria's lands named the *Reichsrat*, and a legislature for Galicia called the *Seim*, were the legislative bodies, elected by adult male voters by a system of mostly indirect elections, but not all men had the vote. The powers of the legislators were set by Austrian law. In practice, Galicia was in many ways autonomous, and the Polish nobility and gentry kept a tight control of political power through gerrymanders, bribery and intimidation. The governor of Galicia was always a Pole. Ukrainians, who called themselves "rusyny" (Ruthenians) or in the mountains a regional name such as "Hutsul" (the subjects of a quite large number of photographs), "Boiko" or "Lemko," had the rights of Austrian citizens, but it was not until the 1890s that they really began to make use of them in the face of the Polish aristocratic domination.

For administrative purposes, Galicia was divided into counties (Ukrainian: *povit*). There were 49 such counties in East Galicia in the 1890s. The principal administrator, and real wielder of power in each county was the county captain (*starosta*), assisted by other bureaucrats and an elected council. The county captain was usually a Pole, as were most of the higher administrators. Below the county were the communes (*hromada*); a commune might be a town or a village or sometimes several villages. Each had a mayor or reeve (*viit*), an elected commune council, and a scribe, who was often a more important personage than the title implies because even in the 1890s a lot of reeves were illiterate. At the village and town level, the councillors were representative of all of East Galicia's peoples—Ukrainians, Poles and Jews. It was at the local or municipal council, and in the elected local school boards, that Ukrainian peasants first obtained valuable experience in politics and self-government.

Because there was practically no Ukrainian nobility and very few "middle class" Ukrainians, the primary leaders of the Ukrainian peasants were for a long time their Greek Catholic priests. The Greek Catholic Church was and is an Eastern-rite Catholic Church, accepting the supremacy of the Pope but with its own ritual and liturgy, and with parish clergy who might be and usually were married men. The Greek Catholics, earlier called "Uniates," and nowadays known as "Ukrainian Catholics," had an Archbishop-Metropolitan in Lviv, and eparchies in Lviv, Peremyshl (now Przemyśl) and Stanyslaviv (now Ivano-Frankivsk).

Many changes were taking place in East Galicia in the late nineteenth century. One important one was in transportation. By the 1890s main railway lines connected East Galicia to the other parts of the Austrian Empire and to western Europe. Already in the mid 1880s the railway reached into such remote parts as Pokuttia and Podillia, and there was extensive construction of branch lines in the 1890s. The volume of agricultural produce carried as well as the amount of passenger traffic increased rapidly, and many small towns and villages soon found themselves no more than a few kilometers from a railway station. Roads, traditionally in poor condition apart from the Imperial highways, began to be used as feeder routes to the railways, and were improved especially in the vicinity of the stations. Postal services became more efficient, and more and more villages and small towns had post and telegraph offices and post office savings banks. By 1900, 22 Galician towns had telephone services.

Villagers had traditionally travelled quite long distances to annual fairs, such as the St. Anne's Fair in Ternopil, and on pilgrimages to places such as Zarvanytsia. Now, instead of walking or riding in a wagon, they were able to travel much faster by train. Often there were special excursion fares to particular events. There were also more and more *viche* (popular assemblies) to discuss matters of interest, attracting hundreds and even thousands of people. Improved transportation meant that the animals that the peasant farmers raised and the crops which they grew could be more easily transported to far-off markets, thereby providing a stimulus to agriculture; it meant, too, that commodities as well as knowledge could more readily flow to the villages from the city and the wider world. The influx of manufactured goods such as textiles had some harmful effects on domestic handicrafts, as well as providing villagers with a far greater choice of goods than ever before. The influx of ideas had an even more profound effect.

Significant changes came to the villages as a result of increasing education opportunities and increasing literacy. Elementary education was in theory compulsory in Galicia from 1868 onwards, but it was not until the 1880s and 1890s that universal schooling really penetrated the predominantly Ukrainian villages. The people taxed themselves to build and maintain elementary schools for their children, often with an attached teacher's residence, and to pay the teacher's salary. In the 1890s many predominantly Ukrainian village schools already had two teachers instead of just one.

The curriculum of the schools (described on page 73) was determined by the Austrian government in Vienna; the language of instruction was supposed to be the regional language of the majority of the children but was decided ultimately by the Galician School Council in Lviv. Because this council was dominated by Poles, Ukrainian village children sometimes began their schooling in the Polish language, though Ukrainian would then also be introduced in grade two. Ukrainians had other grievances against the education system, for it discriminated against them and their language in secondary and higher education, including teacher training. Although the Polish nobility wished village children, Ukrainians and Poles alike, to get just enough schooling to make them literate and able to do simple arithmetic, dedicated teachers often ensured that they received much more. The very high illiteracy rate was being significantly reduced towards the end of the century; in fact schoolchildren in East Galicia had a form of bilingual education, Polish and Ukrainian, and the Canadian immigration agent in Dauphin, Manitoba, was able to attest in 1898 that young Ukrainian men and boys were usually literate in both languages.

Villagers also benefitted in this period from the establishment of popular enlightenment societies such as Prosvita. These societies had as their general aim the promotion of the national and political identity, and the health and well-being of East Galicia's Ukrainians. They published books and pamphlets, in simple language, on a great variety of topics, from beekeeping and better crops to treatment of human and animal diseases, civic rights and how to establish reading clubs. Their members founded newspapers, some of them deliberately designed to appeal to villagers and carrying news from the villages. They formed a consumer cooperative, Narodna Torhivlia, with branches in a number of county towns. Above all, perhaps, they led the movement for the establishment of village reading clubs, where newspapers and books were read—sometimes read aloud to those who could not read— and discussed by villagers, who would thus come to know something of what was happening in Galicia and in the wider world, as well matters of importance to an agricultural community, including grain prices in Lviv and Vienna.

There was a great spurt in the founding of village reading clubs in the 1890s, and some of them branched out into other practical activities, such as organizing credit unions, building village grain storage facilities, and establishing village shops. Reading clubs typically also held commemorative functions, for example in honour of the great Ukrainian poet Taras Shevchenko, and educational and social events. Some organized choirs; at least one village in the 1890s had a brass band. Women could become members of village reading clubs and take part in their events, though the membership remained mostly male.

Village priests often took the lead in organizing village reading clubs, though by the end of the nineteenth century other, secular, Ukrainian

community leaders also emerged: lawyers, teachers, journalists and writers, doctors, as well as some peasants. Moreover, because they were also farmers, East Galicia's Greek Catholic clergy also promoted improved agricultural practices, better breeds of animals, improved seeds. Of one such priest it is told that he gave his parishioners advice on agriculture from the pulpit on Sundays; however, the clergy led by example as well as by exhortation. At a time when European agriculture was in something of a slump, Ukrainian peasants were learning ways to intensify their agriculture, to grow better and more diverse crops, and to make more money from animal husbandry. Even though most of their landholdings were small and their productivity limited in comparison with west European norms, they were increasing production and becoming successful smallholding farmers.

Improved agricultural productivity and its accompanying better nutrition, an increased level of literacy, and more news about the outside world, had other consequences too. Among the information now reaching the villages in newspapers and pamphlets were items dealing with the identification and treatment of disease, and with personal hygiene, including the making of soap. East Galicia shared in the general European movement towards improved personal cleanliness in the last quarter of the nineteenth century. The high death rate began to decline in the 1880s, as did the very high birth rate—both signs of modernization. Vaccination against smallpox was free and compulsory. Outbreaks of cholera, as in 1892, were contained through restrictions on the assembly and movement of people and by the chemical treatment of areas around wells. But there were very few medical doctors or hospitals in the rural areas. Midwives—both those who were officially licensed after taking a midwifery course, and village "wise women" who had learned their skills from their mothers or grandmothers—attended to pre- and post-natal care and to the births themselves, and probably gave other medical advice and treatments.

Mostly the villagers were dependent on their own resources for their health care. Women grew a whole array of medicinal herbs in their gardens, and gathered others in the fields or on the river banks. Local lore, behind which often was practical experience, stipulated the conditions under which such herbs should be picked to ensure the best curative properties. They were carefully dried and stored, to be used when needed, generally during the fall and winter months. Garlic was also much used. Modern science has tended to confirm the curative properties of many of the herbs that were much in use in East Galicia. Village bone-setters often looked after bodily injuries. Sometimes a landowner's or priest's wife had a well-stocked medicine chest as well as some knowledge to put at the disposal of villagers; sometimes a convent with nuns who had some nursing skills was within reach. But mainly villagers relied on their own resilience, now aided by better nutrition, and on age-old remedies for their various illnesses.

If health care still relied mainly on traditional ways, modern ways of thinking entered the village in respect of civic activities and politics. Villagers took part in their own self-government. They also took part in elections to the county councils and to the legislative bodies of Galicia and Austria. Better nourished, somewhat healthier, and economically somewhat better off, as well as better informed, the Ukrainian people of East Galicia took an increased interest in politics. The newspapers and enlightenment societies strove to inform villagers of their rights as Austrian citizens and to affirm their independence from the attitudes of the hitherto dominant Polish nobility. The same sources also promoted the use of the Ukrainian language, the various Ukrainian voluntary associations, an awareness of the villagers' uniquely Ukrainian heritage, and support for Ukrainian candidates at election times. The rural people of East Galicia began to look more confidently to controlling their own lives, most of all at the local level. They became more vocal and active participants in local government; they formed societies to help each other in times of need, insured their properties with a Ukrainian insurance company, and became increasingly self-aware, politically conscious and ultimately nationally conscious. As the villagers' feelings of dignity and self-worth increased, so did their expectations of a better life, for themselves and especially for the next generation. For some of them this would lead to emigration to another country, one with vast stretches of farmland, for they sensed that only in a more developed and open society could these expectations be fulfilled.

Going to the harvest (from Zhydachiv to Berezhnytsia Korolivska

Hutsul villagers carrying logs for the building of a house, Kosiv

House Construction

The village house with its whitewashed walls and golden thatched roof, surrounded by flower gardens and fruit trees, the yard neatly kept and enclosed with a wattled fence, was one of the people's most loved and valued possessions. From earliest times the building of a house was an important milestone in the life of a family. The whole process, from the selection of the location, the construction itself and taking residence in the new dwelling, was accorded a series of different rituals and blessings in order to ensure the strength and security of the new home and a happy and prosperous life within.

The first step in the building of a house was choosing the best location for the dwelling. The site was to be on dry ground, preferably on the side of a hill or in an upland area where no dew would collect in the morning. Places where cattle were once kept, where a family had lived in peace with one another, or where no children had died, were other favourable locations. The sites of former churches or other sacred ground, places where trees grew (especially elder, pear and blackthorn), where people succumbed to disease or epidemic, a crossroads and any location at which a house had been destroyed by lightning were always avoided. Fortune tellers or village elders often advised prospective home owners about the location for the new dwelling. The site would be seeded with oats before the construction began as a means of determining the suitability of their choice. If the oats grew well an appropriate location had been chosen and the work could begin.

The successful outcome of any house building project depended on its beginning and efforts would be taken at the outset to meet various ritualistic requirements—*Dobryi pochatok, to polovyna roboty* (A good beginning is half the work). One of the best ways to ensure this was to begin building on certain days of the week. Tuesday, Thursday, Friday and Saturday were considered to be especially good choices and a house whose construction was begun on these days would ensure for the family a peaceful and prosperous life. The work would never be undertaken on a Monday, Wednesday, or at any time during a leap year. These were regarded as extremely unlucky and houses built during these times would bring misfortune both to the dwelling and its occupants.

The village house (*khata, khalupa*; also *burdey* and *burdiy* among the Hutsuls) was at the same time functional, sturdy, and aesthetically pleasing in form and ornamentation. It was traditionally built from logs and clay, the interior and exterior walls clay-plastered and whitewashed with lime and crowned with a steeply pitched roof made from rye thatch. The house was always built facing southward, both to collect the heat and light from the sun and to protect the entrance from cold north winds. It was warm in winter, cool in summer and, provided that the structure was cared for and maintained, a well-built village house would stand for more than 100 years.

The interior of the village house was almost identical in all parts of Galicia. There were generally two rooms, the living area and the storage room (*komora*), with an unheated porch or entrance (*siny*) between them. The living area of the house was dominated by the clay oven (*pich*) which was always built in the corner of the house facing the door. Furnishings were modest but functional. Typically, a wooden shelf or cupboard for dishes hung by the oven and a table and benches were placed in front

House and Home CHAPTER 2

of the window. Other items would include beds, a chest for clothing, kerosene lamps, holy pictures, embroideries, tapestries and potted plants on the windowsills. The floor was usually made from packed clay although more prosperous peasants were likely to have wooden floors. By the turn of the century prosperous peasants were building larger houses.

The completion of the building of a new house was an important accomplishment and a sign to all of the skill and prosperity of the villager. Chasing a cat or a rooster inside the house previous to moving in was a symbolic means of bringing good luck to the dwelling. The family's eldest member, carrying bread, salt and a bowl filled with a mixture of wheat, rye and some coins, would go into the house the following day to bless each of the four corners and strew the floor with the contents of the bowl to ensure for them a bountiful future. Visits from friends and relatives, offerings of food and drink and a party with music, singing and dancing would follow and traditonally marked the beginning of the family's new life in their new home.

Construction of a village house, Denysiv, Ternopil county

(above) A new house under construction in Denysiv, Ternopil county

(right) A village woman taking new window frames to the glazier in Zhydachiv

(above) House building in Galicia began to employ more modern methods of construction beginning in the last decades of the 1800s as seen in this house nearing completion in Zhydachiv. Wooden framing and planks took the place of logs to form the walls and a shingled roof replaced the thatch. While changes such as these were taking place, the traditional log house remained popular and was still being widely built.

(above right) Village house, Zhydachiv

(right) A Hutsul-style house with a wooden shingled roof near Kosiv

The house of a *zahorodnyk*, Zabolotivtsi, Zhydachiv county

The term *zahorodnyk* (gardener) was used to designate one category of peasant. A person with this designation, such as the villager in this photograph, possessed his own house and garden but no other land. He was a landless labourer who made his living from a means other than farming his own land. A villager who earned his income from a trade or craft rather than farming was usually a *zahorodnyk*.

A village farmstead, Berezhnytsia Korolivska, Zhydachiv county

The Farm Yard

Several types of structures were found on the Galician farm yard. The most common in addition to the house were storage buildings, shelters for the animals, sheds, wells and various types of fences. All of the buildings were of log construction with rooves made of thatch, wood or tin. Plaitwork was found in village architecture but was extremely archaic and used only for some of the smaller farmstead structures.

The threshing barn (*stodola, klunia*), the largest of the storage buildings, was used for keeping unthreshed grain, hay and straw for the animals, and it served as a place for threshing the sheaves and drying and bagging the harvest after winnowing. The walls were usually left unplastered with the spaces between the logs providing the necessary ventilation. Some farmers made a threshing floor of firmly packed clay directly in front of the barn on which the grain was spread and beaten with a flail. While the *stodola* usually stood as a separate building in the farm yard it could be connected with the stable, granary (*komora*) and the house under a single roof.

The granary (*komora*) was a place for keeping grain, flour, winter clothing, agricultural implements and equipment for the horses. In some regions it was called a *shpikhler*. Hutsuls referred to it as an *ambar*. While other farm buildings had no proper ceiling or floor, this building was relatively finished. A young married couple living with the husband's parents typically slept in the *komora* during the summer months. When detached from the dwelling as a separate building it was always built in such a place that it could be seen from the windows of the house.

The cornhouse (*koshnytsia*) was used to store unhusked cobs of corn and was a regular feature of the village farmsteads of the southwestern areas of Podillia and Pokuttia where maize was grown as a principal field crop. The *koshnytsia* was distinctive, having a circular, oval or four-sided wooden framework raised off the ground on a wooden or stone foundation and wattled from wicker. It was covered with a thatched roof but the walls were left unplastered to allow for air circulation.

To store root vegetables and salted foods for the winter, the family dug a *lokh* or root cellar. It was in the yard or garden (never inside the house), sometimes lined with boards and straw and topped with a wooden cover. Wealthier peasants and those living on the estates would have cellars of masonry construction with special fitted covers.

Animal husbandry was an integral part of the agriculture of Ukrainians of East Galicia and required certain basic buildings. The stable (*staynia*) was where the cattle and horses were kept and often had a fenced area in front of the building where the animals were kept during the day. There was a sty (*kucha, khliv*) for the hogs, which sometimes also served as a pen for the ducks and geese, and a coop for the chickens. The chicken coop (*kurnyk*) was customarily built facing the windows of the house and set off the ground on a wooden or stone foundation. Like the *koshnytsia*, it was wattled from wicker, covered with a coating of clay plaster and capped with a thatched roof. A sheepfold (*koshara*) or another similar pen or enclosure typically completed the built inventory of the Galician farm yard.

Typical village farmstead with enclosure, Stryhantsi, Tovmach county

A village farmstead, Tyshkivtsi, Horodenka county

The threshing barn of a noble family, Dovhe, Tovmach county

Manor House

In Galicia most villages had an estate or manor (*dvir*). These were large landholdings where the lord of the local manor lived, often only from time to time. The manor estate could include one or more farmsteads (*filvarky*) in the vicinity of the village, numerous buildings and usually a fine residence. The estates were generally owned by Polish nobles, gentry or other wealthy families, some of whom had a long history of settlement, land ownership and control in the East Galician countryside.

The residences of the manor lord (*pan*) differed greatly from those of the peasants. They varied from elegant stone palaces to modest frame houses with many rooms. Large windows, balconies, fireplaces or tiled stoves and numerous items of furniture, both of domestic and imported manufacture, distinguished them from village peasant houses. The grounds of the manor house usually boasted beautifully tended gardens with pathways, flowers beds and ornamental hedges. A stone wall or high fence typically demarcated the property of the village manor. Living quarters for the servants and labourers as well as various agricultural buildings, mills, distilleries, breweries or brickyards which the manor operated were also part of the estate buildings.

Manor lords and their families led separate and very different lives from the villagers. Occasional religious and cultural festivities might bring them together for a brief time every year, but as a rule the class distinction was quite rigidly maintained. Not all of the landlords were disinterested in the villagers' lives, and some of their wives could be very generous, providing medical and other assistance to them in times of need. Certain landlords were renowned for their philanthropy and donations of land or money for the building of churches or schools. Some, like the Sapieha family, founded orphanages and cultural organizations or otherwise assisted the people with gifts, monetary loans or donations in kind. In return the peasants treated them with deference if not with affection.

Manor house in Voltsniv, Zhydachiv county

Wells

The well (*kolodiaz*, *studnia*, *krynytsia*, *kernytsia*) was an important part of the village farmstead. Its primary function was to provide the villagers with a source of water for their domestic use. During the summer months it also served as a place where perishable foods such as milk, cream and butter were kept cool. The whole area had a relatively high ground water table and adequate rainfall, especially in the Carpathian mountains and foothills region. Mineral springs were found in all parts of Galicia as were artesian wells which flowed year round.

Wells were constructed by individuals or by the community as a whole. For villagers who did not have their own wells, they always had access to the community well and to the river or stream that ran nearby. Some village men specialized in welldigging and were hired by others to dig and build the structure. The cribbing was made from wooden boards, typically pine or spruce but never poplar, which imparted a bitter taste to the water. In some areas the cribbing was also made from stone.

In shallow wells where the ground water was found relatively close to the surface the water was drawn out using a bucket and a wooden pole with a hook attached to the end. For deeper wells a lifting lever, a *zhuravel*, or a pulley, was used to draw the water with a rope and bucket. Wells in the form of shallow ponds or pools (*kopanky*) were cribbed with a discarded *zhlukto* (a type of wooden tub), *kadovb* (beehive) or a wooden barrel with the bottom removed. Hutsul villagers used a large hollowed out tree stump which was set over the water source as a form of cribbing.

On various occasions the well was the site for the performance of certain rites and rituals. The blessing of the water on *Yordan* or the floating of plaited wreaths by young women as a part of the fortune telling games of *Kupalo* often took place at the well. A piece of bread was tossed into the well water and allowed to soak overnight as a symbolic means of preventing a witch from stealing the milk from a cow. It was removed the following day, blessed with the required phrases and fed to the cow, an action which was believed to keep the witch at a distance and protect the animal from harm.

In the villages the community well was the responsibility of the local authorities. If it was neglected or poorly maintained, it could contribute to the spread of disease, especially cholera, and village officials were continually reminded of the importance of properly cribbed and clean community wells. Wells which were in disrepair were to be reconstructed or new ones built. Most villages in Galicia had community wells and they were an amenity to which all of the people had access.

Going to the well for water, Tyshkivtsi, Horodenka county

Drawing water from the well, Tyshkivtsi, Horodenka county

Fences

The fences served a practical and decorative function on the village farms. They were used to demarcate a pen or pasture where farm animals would be kept for the night. They were built around vegetable and flower gardens so as to keep the cattle or chickens from eating or trampling the plants. Most importantly they were erected around the yard or between fields as a sign of property ownership. In all cases the fences were an attractive and characteristic component of the village farmstead. Unlike among some other Slavic people, such as the Russians who typically did not fence their yards, it was considered highly improper for the yard of a Ukrainian villager to be left unfenced.

There were several different types of fences and they differed in both form and the materials used in their construction. Wattled fences (*ploty*, *pleteni tyny*) were the predominant type in the forest and forest-steppe areas of East Galicia. These were made by driving a row of wooden poles into the ground at even intervals along the perimeter of the area of be fenced. Rods of young willow or hazel, cut by the villager himself or purchased at the market, were then woven or wattled horizontally around the poles, often producing intricate patterns or designs. A popular variation of the wattling technique used thin rails which were attached to posts at the top and midway points around which the roads were wattled vertically.

Fences were constructed from flagstone or other types of flat rock in areas with relatively few trees but an abundance of rock and stone. Fences built from wooden posts and flat boards (*parkany*) were especially common in the forested areas of East Galicia and on wealthier farmsteads throughout the region. All of the fences had gates of various types and styles which ranged from simple wooden constructions to more elaborate structures made from iron or grille work.

Villagers wattling a fence, Zhydachiv

Hauling manure to the fields, Denysiv, Ternopil county

In the Fields

Agriculture remained the most important occupation in East Galicia until well into the twentieth century. In the last decades of the 1800s, however, a transition was taking place in the countryside with the introduction of new crops, improvements in farming methods and an increased emphasis on animal husbandry. These developments were changing the ways the peasants thought about and did their agricultural work and the older ways, while still in use, were being replaced by new methods.

As in all primarily agricultural societies, the fieldwork had a certain rhythm to its performance. The farmers followed a calendar of their own with cycles and seasons, each regulated by folk customs and traditonal practises. Many were also engaged in supplementary occupations. Some of the work was harder than others but the villagers were not discontented with the demands made on their physical and mental energies. On many occasions they worked on a task together—in the fields, threshing grain or husking corn—and celebrated its completion communally.

The work in the fields began with the preparation of the soil and the seeding of the spring crops. Custom dictated that the new agricultural season could begin only after the Feast of the Annunciation (*Blahovishchennia*) and previous to this any working of the soil was considered to be a sin. The land was fertilized and ploughed and the grain sown by hand in a broadcast motion. Lighter-weight grains, such as oats, rye and barley, were seeded in the following manner using three handfuls of grain per step: one thrown to the right, one in front and one to left of the farmer as he walked across the furrows. Heavier-weight grains, such as wheat, were seeded using two handfuls per step: one thrown to the front and one to the left. A harrow or large tree branch was dragged over the field to cover the grain upon completion. Because the villagers' landholdings were generally quite small, the use of equipment for seeding was not practical. Seeding by hand, however, was being replaced by mechanical methods in all areas of the region by the late nineteenth century.

The principal crops grown by landlords and peasants alike were wheat (in many varieties), rye, barley, oats, potatoes, millet, buckwheat and beans. Cash crops such as lentils, peas, poppy seed, turnips, tobacco, hemp and flax were also cultivated, especially by peasants for whom it was cost effective on their smaller landholdings. Maize was especially common in the Carpathian

regions where flour and meal made from ground corn was a staple in the diet of the Hutsuls. Sugar beets were being cultivated for sale in some areas. Many different kinds of vegetables were planted in the gardens: garlic, onions, beets, cabbage, cucumbers, melons, pumpkin and radishes. Some villagers also grew hops and grapes. Fruit culture was extremely popular in Galicia and so every household would have an orchard with apple, pear, cherry, plum or walnut trees.

Because agriculture was the central means of making a living, the peasants sought to have at least a modicum of control over the elements and maintained various beliefs to see themselves through the hardships of farming. It was inevitable too that besides prayers there would be superstitions connected to every phase of the work in the fields. Agriculture was their livelihood and to ensure success in their work various measures would be invoked. It was considered bad luck among the Ukrainian villagers to begin any type of agricultural work on a Tuesday or Saturday or at any time during a full moon. The Hutsuls believed that to step over a tool or implement which was being used in the field would foretell rain and hail

Working the Land CHAPTER 3

damage to the crop. An especially superstitious farmer would neither eat nor bring any food with him while working in the fields as a symbolic means of preventing the birds from eating the grain.

In order to increase the productivity of their cropland and gardens the villagers used manure as fertilizer which they hauled from their farm yards and spread on the fields. The increase in the number of domestic animals towards the end of the nineteenth century assured a greater supply of manure. Chemical fertilizers were also introduced at this time. Manure hauling was often done communally in the form of a work bee (*toloka*) which might include a group of farmers in a particular village and culminate with a party afterward with music and dancing.

(above) Preparing the field for planting, Denysiv, Ternopil county

(above right) Sorting potatoes before seeding, Denysiv, Ternopil county

(right) Preparations for seeding the field, Zarohyzno, Zhydachiv county

(left) Sowing the grain, Zarohyzno, Zhydachiv county

(above) Sorting broadbeans in a sieve, Tyshkivtsi, Horodenka county

A group of villagers going from Zhydachiv to Zarohyzno to cut hay

haying

Hay cutting (*sinokis*) usually began around the middle of June after the work of preparing and seeding the grain fields had been completed. The work started early in the day as soon as the dew had evaporated with the cutters using a scythe (*kosa*) in a rhythmical swinging motion to cut the hay. It was a slow process and one which demanded not only the physical strength but also the skill and endurance of the cutter. Of all Slavs Ukrainians were said to be the best hay cutters.

After it was cut the hay was raked into rows, called windrows (*kopytsi*), and left on the field to dry. The windrows were then turned with pitchforks the following day to allow the hay to dry uniformly. If the weather was favourable the hay was ready for storage in the afternoon of the day following the cutting. It was hauled by wagon loads into the farm yard and piled into haystacks (*kopy*) where it would be left and used as needed, sometimes enclosed with a wattled fence in order to keep the farm animals from damaging or knocking them down.

Proper drying or curing (referred to as field-curing) was necessary for the efficient preservation of the hay for the winter. Fermentation processes which reduced its nutritional value, especially the quantity of carbohydrates, would take place if it were not dried soon after harvesting. Excessive drying, on the other hand, would result in a loss of protein and so the curing process was attended to carefully.

In the Carpathian region the Hutsuls made hay twice a year: in July around St. Ivan's Day, called *sino ivanichne*, and in the fall around the beginning of September during the Feast of the Virgin Mary (*Bohorodytsia*), called *bohorodychne sino*. The hay was placed on poles to dry instead of being raked into windrows because of the frequent rains in the mountain areas. The poles (*koly*) were made from straight spruce trees which were cut and trimmed of most of their branches, leaving only the thicker limbs as hooks from which to hang the hay. The bottoms of the trunks were sharpened with an axe so that they could be driven securely into the ground.

The hay was removed from the poles after it had dried sufficiently and piled into a haystack where it would remain until needed. The Hutsul farmer often placed a *kil* (singular of *koly*) in the centre when making the haystack as a means of providing additional support. A layer of rocks or spruce branches placed on the ground underneath would help to keep the hay dry. Additional protection was provided by driving four poles in the ground around the perimeter of the haystack from which a thatched roof would be suspended, and which could be raised or lowered, to keep off the rain.

Nettles were sometimes used as a substitute feed for farm animals and poultry during times when hay was scarce. It made an excellent fodder that was rich in minerals and protein and was known by the farmers to increase milk production and egg yields. Other herbs and wild plants served as feed for the animals though wormwood (*polyn*) would never be fed to the cattle because it gave a bitter taste to the milk.

A young man carrying *koly* to the field, Rozhniativ, Dolyna county

(below) A hay-cutter cleaning his scythe, Zabolotivtsi, Zhydachiv county

(right) Drying alfalfa, Kosiv

(below right) Carrying hay in an *opalka* (a net made from ropes), Bolekhiv

ᴃringing in the Crops

Na Illi novyi khlib na stoli (The first bread of the harvest is on the table by St. Illia's day). In most areas of Galicia the harvest began in summer and was completed by St. Illia's Day on July 15. Although both men and women participated in the field labour, harvesting was traditionally considered to be women's work. Their dominant role in this process, especially in the tasks of reaping, binding and stacking the sheaves, was reflected in many of the rites and rituals of the harvest season (see also *Obzhynky*).

The ripened grain was cut with a sickle (*serp*) and bound into sheaves (*snopy*) using bands of freshly cut straw. They were placed into shocks consisting of 60 sheaves (*kopy*) and half-shocks of 30 sheaves (*polukipky*) and left to dry in the field. Both the *kopa* and *polukipok* were built by placing the sheaves in the form of an X with the heads of the grain pointing upward. The top was covered with the *shapka*, an additional sheaf which functioned in much the same way as the thatched roof in directing rain water off the sheaves below. Traditionally the work in the field was done to the singing of ritual harvest songs or the accompaniment of music.

In the Hutsul region the sheaves were hung on the wooden poles to dry. The wet conditions of the mountain areas prevented the placing of any of the harvested grain directly on the ground. The poles typically held between 15 and 20 sheaves each and were covered on top with the protective *shapka*. The sheaves were removed when they had dried sufficiently and taken to the farm yard where they were stored in the barn or outside under a cover of spruce branches until threshing time.

Threshing, the process of beating the sheaves with a flail (*tsip*) in order to separate the grain from the chaff, was done on the floor of the threshing barn or left until winter when the sheaves were taken outside and beaten on a patch of ice or firmly packed snow. This portion of the harvest work was usually performed by men. The straw was raked away, the grain shovelled into a pile and then winnowed by tossing it into the air using a large wire-meshed sieve called a *resheto*. The lighter weight chaff straw was carried away in the wind leaving the heavier grain to fall to the ground. The cleaned grain was spread out in the sun to dry before being bagged and stored in the *komora* or *stodola*. Stamp mills (*stupy*), the hand operated *zhorny* or the wind and water mills which were widespread in all parts of Galicia were used by the villagers to mill the grain.

Stacks (*polukipky*) of barley sheaves, Rozhniativ, Dolyna county

Harvesting to the accompaniment of music, Berezhnytsia Korolivska, Zhydachiv county

(above left) At home on the yard, putting the brake on the wagon, Stryhantsi, Dolyna county

(above) Drying the wheat sheaves, Tyshkivtsi, Horodenka county

(left) Preparing to thresh the grain, Tyshkivtsi, Horodenka county

(above) Threshing the barley with a flail, Tyshkivtsi, Horodenka county

(above right) Collecting the threshed grain, Tyshkivtsi, Horodenka county

(right) Drying the threshed grain on the yard, Tyshkivtsi, Horodenka county

Piling up the sugar beets, Zarohyzno, Zhydachiv county

On their way to the potato field, Hnizdychiv, Zhydachiv county

The Potato Harvest

Potatoes (*kartoplia, barabolia, bulba; buryishka* among the Hutsuls), often called the "second bread" by the Ukrainians, were a staple in the diet of the village family. While traditionally cultivated as a garden crop in Galicia, the amount of ploughland devoted to the growing of potatoes increased in the 1890s. They were a good source of protein and different varieties were being introduced steadily into Galicia. They were especially favoured by the Hutsuls who described them as *ni molotyty, ni do mlyna a prosto do horshka* (they require neither threshing nor milling but simply go right into the pot). Potatoes were also being used as feed for farm animals, especially those which were not fit for planting.

The potatoes were brought into the house from the *komora* or *stodola* two or three weeks before beginning the spring planting. Still in their bags, they were placed in the kitchen or under one of the beds and allowed to warm up before being sorted. The field was ploughed and the soil left for a few days to be warmed by the sun after which holes were dug with a spade or hoe and the potatoes seeded by hand. In many areas planting the potatoes concluded the spring work in the fields.

The potato harvest took place in early to mid September in East Galicia. Women and men worked together during this harvest as well, although if working for the *pan* women usually earned a lesser wage. The potatoes were dug with forks and hoes and left to dry before bagging or piling them in baskets and bringing them in from the fields to be sorted. The larger ones were kept for eating, the medium-sized ones were set aside for seed for the following year and the small ones were fed to the hogs. The labourers were also responsible for cleaning the potato field at the end of the harvest and the uprooted plants would be piled and later burned. Like the grain harvest, the work in the potato fields was often done to the accompaniment of music or singing.

As potatoes came to be seeded more extensively as a field crop, the peasants were offered much in the way of practical advice with regards to their cultivation. Agricultural columns in the Galician press advised the farmers to be cautious in their choice of seed potatoes for planting. Firm, medium-sized ones were said to produce the greatest yield. Those which had sprouted were not to be used because the shoots would break off during the planting process. Cutting the potatoes into smaller pieces before planting was also not recommended as it deprived the young plants of vital nutrients during their initial growing stages. An inexpensive but effective means of fertilizing potato plants was to sprinkle them with a mixture of salt and powdered wood ashes.

Digging potatoes, Zhydachiv

At the Hutsul blacksmith's shop, Kosiv

The traditional view of the society of East Galicia from which Ukrainians came to Canada has seen them as a uniformly agricultural folk. Some recognition has been given to the fact that the immigrants had a variety of other skills yet the overall picture has tended to ignore their diverse occupational abilities.

Blacksmithing

The villagers' demand for iron goods was satisfied by the local blacksmith. There was usually a smithy in every village, run either by a man with a thorough training in the working of metal or by a self-taught peasant. Blacksmithing was one of the oldest trades practiced by Ukrainian men and in many blacksmiths' families the occupation passed from father to son over several generations.

As a general rule the village blacksmith worked on a commission basis. Some craftsmen, particularly those who lived and worked in the larger towns

Tanning

Although tanning was practised by Ukrainians throughout East Galicia, the Hutsuls were especially well-known for their working of leather. One of the most important areas for this activity was the town of Bolekhiv and its craftsmen were sought throughout the region for the high quality of their workmanship in producing a wide assortment of leather and leather-made goods.

Hutsul tanners used a variety of techniques for the making of leather, each depending on the individual animal skin and the purpose for which the leather would be used. Leather intended for the making of boots, for example, would be treated differently from that for harnesses or collars. The raw skins, after they were removed from the slaughtered animal and dried in the sun, were cured by a process of salting or brine-curing in which the skins were soaked in tubs containing a flour and salt water solution.

Supplementary Occupations CHAPTER 4

and urban centres, manufactured a whole inventory of products which were sold at the markets and fairs. They made tools and agricultural implements such as axes, hatchets, hoes, sickles, scythes, ploughs, chisels, horseshoes and fish hooks using local or imported metals. They manufactured locks, keys, hinges, latches and other closing devices, tinder boxes, oil lamps, candle holders, tripods for setting pots over an open fire and grills. Also among their repertory were religious objects such as iron crosses which were set on top of wooden roadside crosses, graves, and on church towers. Many blacksmiths were skilled in making jewellery and small decorative items such as rings and buttons from copper, brass and silver. They provided other services, such as shoeing horses, and were often sought by the villagers to repair tools or implements.

The working of metal was practised from earliest times among the Hutsuls. They, more than other Ukrainian peoples, were extremely creative in their craft and were known for the rich ornamentation and design in their work. The intricate nature and high artistic quality of the items produced testified to the level of technology and the talent of these blacksmiths. The market-town of Kosiv in the Hutsul region was one of the major centres of the blacksmith trade in all of Galicia.

In preparation for the tanning, the cured skins were rinsed in fresh water to remove the salt and any traces of blood and dirt, and to replace moisture which was lost during the curing process. After they had soaked for as long as seven days, the flesh was removed from the inner surface by scraping with a special blunt knife called a *shkafa*. The skins were subsequently immersed in a solution of lime, wood ashes and water which would remove the hair and complete the last of the prepatory steps.

Tanning the hides was done by soaking the stock in tubs containing successively stronger tannin solutions, usually for several weeks at a time. More tannin would be added to the solution to increase the concentration until the hides absorbed sufficient quantities to complete the tanning process. The leather was then lubricated with soap or grease and stretched into shape. The tannin required by the craftsmen was extracted from the bark of various trees, especially oak, cherry and willow which had a high content of the substance occurring naturally. The bark was boiled in water, sometimes with the addition of other ingredients, to prepare the tanning solution.

Soaking the hides in water before working them, Bolekhiv, Dolyna county

Drying a fine crop of tobacco under the eaves of a village house, Tyshkivtsi, Horodenka county

Cultivation of Specialty Crops

The growing of specialty crops was very profitable with many farmers earning their largest annual income from these crops. Where the climate was favourable, the growing of tobacco was advantageous for villagers despite the fact that sale of tobacco was a state monopoly. Once the preserve of the large landowners, it came to be concentrated in peasant hands because of its labour-intensive nature. Specialty tobaccos were also grown, such as those which were favoured by the gentry for which the villagers knew there would be a guaranteed market. Other types of commercial specialty crops included poppy seed, anise, fennel and caraway, the production of which even small amounts of these crops could substantially supplement the peasants' earnings.

Beekeeping

Beekeeping was a traditional secondary occupation among the village farmers. In earlier times honey was obtained from wild bees which nested in trees, rock gorges or in primitive beehives which the villagers constructed from hollow logs or tree stumps. As the trade developed and the demand for honey increased more sophisticated wooden hives (*vulyky*) were built. Apiaries (*pasiky*), covered with thatched or planked rooves and enclosed by a fence, protected the hives from the elements and bears or other forest animals. In areas where wood was in short supply, beehives were plaited from straw or willows and plastered with clay.

Honey had long been important in the lives of the people. It was the main sweetening agent in their diet and appeared extensively in folk medicine where it was especially known for its heeling attributes. It was also used as a moistening agent in the processing of tobacco. Honey was produced for domestic consumption and for sale at the markets and fairs in its most popular varieties of buckwheat, clover and linden. In the late 1890s a kilogram of honey sold for about 1 crown. An average Galician beekeeper would have approximately 10–15 hives although it was not uncommon for some of the men to keep as many as 100. Towards the end of the century honey was losing its primary place as a sweetener to sugar and there was a reduction in the number of beehives in East Galicia.

There were numerous beliefs and superstitions connected to bees and beekeeping. According to custom the beekeeper would walk around his apiary three times during the day on Good Friday in order to ensure that his bees would always return to their hives. Wreaths of flowers which had been blessed at the church on Corpus Christi were placed inside the apiary or around the hives to provide for the family an abundance of honey. Village apiculturalists knew that the secret to keeping contented bees was to distance the hives from the smell of garlic, laundry hung outside to dry, and barking dogs, all believed to anger the bees and cause them to sting.

Beehives, Bolekhiv

Different types of hand-woven baskets on the potato field, Zabolotivtsi, Zhydachiv county

basketweaving and Plaitwork

The crafts of basketweaving and plaitwork were well developed among the Ukrainians of East Galicia. Woven and plaited objects were widely used, especially as storage vessels and for carrying or transporting goods. Popular items included baskets for sowing grain and for gathering fruits and vegetables; bags, sieves, colanders, fishing traps, nets, hats and footwear. The work of basketweavers and plaiters was also evident in the manufacture of the bodies and linings of carts and wagons, beehives, cradles and chair seats, and in the construction of plaited walls in some farm buildings.

The basic materials used by craftsmen were the branches and runners of young trees such as hazel, alder, juniper and pine, and the bast of linden and elm trees. Thin planks and battens torn from spruce, straw, bullrush, reeds and animal hair were also used. The Hutsuls made baskets from the roots of fir trees for gathering and transporting berries although in general the craft was not as well developed in the Hutsul region as it was in other areas of East Galicia.

Because of the variety of raw materials used by the craftsmen, there were necessarily also many different techniques of weaving and plaiting. Despite the fact that the majority of the manufactured items were utilitarian in purpose, they exhibited great artistic quality in their shape, proportion, texture and colour. The weaver would often incorporate two different types of raw materials, usually of different colours, textures and thicknesses, in order to make them more aesthetically appealing.

As a popular secondary occupation, basketweaving and plaitwork were practised by villagers who occasionally made baskets and other items for their own use and also by those who produced them on commission for others. A large group of these craftsmen operated on a professional basis and sold their products at markets and fairs.

Young boys plaiting rye straw to be used for making hats, Zabolotivtsi, Zhydachiv county

A greaseman selling wagon grease, Nezvyshchi, Horodenka county

The Greaseman

Travelling through the countryside, walking beside his horse and wagon and calling out "*Maz! Maz! Maz!*" ("Grease! Grease! Grease!"), the greaseman was a familiar sight in the towns and villages of East Galicia. His clothing typically stained with the product he was peddling, he would come into the yard and bow before the farmer as he offered his grease for sale. During the winter months, with little need for wagon grease among the farmers, he continued to make his rounds, this time selling the thicker and more expensive grease which was used for polishing leather boots and shoes. In this society where metal equipment was coming to be in greater use, there was a growing need for lubricating oil and this need was met by the greaseman.

The centre for the grease trade in Galicia was the area around the town of Krystynopil. There were numerous grease factories which manufactured and supplied the product and for several weeks of work the average greaseman could expect to earn a respectable income. In 1890 a two hectolitre barrel of grease could be bought for approximately 19 gulden (about $10) and then resold for 18–20 kreuzer (about 8–10 cents) per litre. Most greasemen were typically farmers or gardeners for whom selling grease provided a significant supplemental income.

The wagons used by the greasemen were narrow, often with *drabynky* or ladder-type structures at the front and sides. The grease barrel was set towards the back of the wagon. There was also a smaller barrel of the grease used for polishing boots, a sack of oats for the horse, and hanging from the side of the wagon was a set of graduated metal pots used for measuring and dispensing the grease. The barrel containing the grease usually had a tap near the bottom to decant the grease and another on top to allow air inside which made for a smoother operation.

From Peat to *Palyvo*

The conversion of peat into a usable fuel was one of the many small-scale extractive industries which were beginning to emerge in East Galicia during the late 1800s. It had long been used as a fuel (*palyvo*) in addition to wood and straw, not only in Galicia but also in other European countries, particularly Ireland. With the shortage of wood in many areas of the plains, peat was a viable substitute both for heating and cooking.

Peat was found throughout the entire Ukrainian ethnographical region. The greatest deposits were in Polissia but peat bogs were also found in the marshy river valleys of East Galicia and the swampy soils of the Carpathian foothills. Farmers used it as an organic fertilizer for plants. Because of its excellent moisture-retaining qualities peat was an effective garden mulch and for leguminous plants, especially peas, a thin layer would be spread on the fields after they had sprouted in order to protect the young seedlings from frost. It was also used as a bedding for livestock and for packing and transporting eggs.

(above right) Workmen extracting the peat, Berezhnytsia Korolivska, Zhydachiv county

(right) Transporting the peat to be processed, Berezhnytsia Korolivska, Zhydachiv county

Burning limestone, Stryhantsi, Tovmach county

Burning Limestone

Galicia was rich in deposits of limestone and there were quarries in various locales throughout the region. When burned (raised to a high temperature), it produced lime, a white powdery substance which was used in the preparation of cements and mortars, as a neutralizer of acidic soils in agriculture, and in the manufacture of paper and glass. The villagers used it to make whitewash for their houses and to treat animal hides during the tanning of leather. In folk medicine a mixture of chopped straw and lime would be boiled in water, the vapours from which were inhaled as a treatment for typhus. Eggs would be soaked in a mixture of lime and water to form a protective seal around the shells which would keep them fresh.

Other Occupations

Alongside their primary work in agriculture, some villagers were also engaged in other occupations. These might include cart and wheel making, cooperage, quarrying, fishing, cobbling and candlemaking.

A village cooper, Stryhantsi, Tovmach county

Feeding the fowl, Yaikivtsi, Zhydachiv county

Women in East Galicia, like those in all agricultural societies, worked hard. But here they had an independence and status not often associated with women at that time.

Managing the Household

Zhinocha robota nikoly ne liahala spaty (A woman's work was never done). From early morning until late at night the average day for a village woman consisted of a myriad of tasks, those traditionally considered to be women's work: planting and tending the vegetable garden, harvesting its produce and preserving food for the winter; cooking the meals, washing the dishes; cultivating and working the flax and hemp; spinning, weaving and sewing of clothes; tending the cattle, poultry and pigs; washing and mending clothes, keeping house and, as the main caregiver of the children, raising the family. Many women were also involved in secondary or seasonal occupations. At other times they worked alongside the men, especially during the harvest.

In the last decades of the 1800s, the traditional image of women was changing. They continued in their main tasks of managing the household and raising the children but their contributions were also noted beyond the hearth and home. They began to play a greater public role in society as teachers and in reading clubs, they formed women's organizations and were active participants in debates, lectures and public assemblies.

Wash Day

One of the biggest jobs facing the Galician housewife was the washing of the family's clothes. This was typically done once a week, usually on Monday—folk custom forbade the activity on Wednesday and Friday—and was a task which took up most of her day. In most villages wooden benches (*kladky dlia prannia*) were constructed on the river bank or in the shallow waters of a lake or pond for the purposes of washing clothes. Alternately the laundry was done in wooden tubs at home on the yard.

Several different methods were used for washing clothes. Delicate items of clothing, such as the various types of women's headdress and those adorned with embroidery, were washed gently by hand while those of a heavier weight, such as work clothes, bed linen and table covers, were trampled with the feet or pounded clean with wooden battledores (*pranyky*). The items were then rinsed, wrung out and taken home where they were hung or spread outside to dry. Cloth made from natural fibres tended to become stiff and coarse after washing and so the garments were pressed with the use of a wooden mangle (*maglivnytsia*). More delicate items, such as the women's *namitka* or other types of headgear, would be smoothed with the use of a *halo*, a stone or glass ball about the size of a large orange which was rolled back and forth over the slightly dampened item as it was held by the corners.

Lye, fat-based soaps and those made from organic substances were the commonly used cleaning agents on wash day. Lye was perhaps the most popular because of the ready availability of wood ash from which it was made. In one method a solution was prepared in advance by soaking large

A Woman's Work CHAPTER 5

Girls collecting poppy seed, Tyshkivtsi, Horodenka county

A village woman doing laundry at home on the yard, Tyshkivtsi, Horodenka county

quantities of ashes in hot water. The lye mixture was then strained, diluted to the appropriate concentration and then poured over the clothing in a wooden tub and let to soak for several hours. The items were rinsed with fresh water and pounded with the *pranyk* before being hung or spread to dry.

A similar method for preparing the lye involved the use of a specially constructed wooden vessel *(zhlukto)* on top of which was placed a layer of straw, the item of clothing to be laundered and a sheet or cloth bag sprinkled with wood ashes. A large supply of hot water was prepared nearby which was then poured slowly over top, in the process leaching the lye from the ashes and filtering through the sheet to clean the item of clothing underneath. The *zhlukto* was equipped with a spout at the bottom which allowed the liquid to be collected and poured through the clothing in repeated applications until it was cleaned.

Soap for laundering clothes was purchased in the stores or at the markets and fairs. It was also made by the village women who, in one method of preparation, cooked together beef bones, fat and wood ashes, strained the mixture and then poured it into a flat wooden tray to cool. Organic substances, such as various types of plants and flowers, produced another type of cleaning agent. The herb soapwort, called *tatarske mylo, sobache mylo* or *dyke mylo* by the villagers, when bruised and agitated or boiled in water raised a lather like soap because of the high percentage of natural saponin which it contained. It was well known among village women for its beneficial action on the protein of silk and wool and was especially effective for washing out grease stains and whitening linen fabrics. Used with a suitable mordant, soapwort could also be used to dye silk and wool.

To prepare the soap, quantities of the fresh or dried herb (and in some areas also the dried root) were tied in a cloth bag and boiled in water until foam appeared and the water turned a greenish colour. The item to be laundered was first soaked in cold water to extract as much of the loose dirt as possible and then laid on a wooden board as the soapy froth was worked gently over the surface with the hands. This process was continued and fresh foam applied until there was no longer any dirt left in the material. When the item was clean, the foam would be wiped away and the garment dabbed off with towels and left to dry in a cool, shaded place. In addition to soapwort, extracts of lesser spearwort, baby's-breath and burstwort were also used as soap on wash day.

Earthenware dishes for sale, Zhydachiv market

Markets were a central part of the economic and social life in East Galicia. As one of the traditional and much loved gathering places of the people, a trip to the market was an anticipated and exciting event for the whole family. They were noisy, colourful, crowded, teeming with activity and full of new and wonderful things to be seen and enjoyed. To make purchases, sell goods or simply to socialize and partake of the exotic and appealing atmosphere, there was no better place than the market.

The markets (*yarmarky*, sing. *yarmarok*, from the German *Jahrmarkt* meaning "yearly market") were held annually throughout the entire region, usually coinciding with a feast date on the church calendar from which they took their names. They were held outdoors in cities, towns and villages and lasted from one day to several weeks. In many cases they were not only annual events but were organized several times during the year and attracted upwards of thousands of people. Other types of markets, the *torhy* (sing. *torh*), were held once or twice a week in the towns specially licensed for this purpose and were organized on a smaller scale. These served generally a local retail function where villagers and small estate owners would sell their agricultural produce and locally produced handicraft items and buy what they needed.

To Market to Market CHAPTER 6

A typical East Galician market tempted the people with a wide assortment of goods. There was a selection of food-stuffs including grain in its many varieties, vegetables, fresh and preserved fruits and berries, honey, butter, lard, rice, salt, fish, sugar and alcohol. Handicraft items made from wood, pottery, fur, leather, wool and wicker were for sale as were agricultural implements, feathers, horsehair, wood and building materials, hay, tobacco, tallow and candles. Cartwrights, wheelwrights, coopers and blacksmiths displayed their wares and demonstrated their crafts. Tailors laid out textiles and different garments while brass and silversmiths tempted onlookers with jewellery, buttons, goblets and ornamental crosses. Cattle, horses and other domestic animals added to the inventory of goods for sale. Services, such as those of photographers, butchers, bakers, restauranteurs and tavern-keepers, were provided, as was the entertainment of jugglers, magicians and concert and theatre performances.

The markets offered many goods from outside the region in addition to those which were produced and manufactured locally. Tea, coffee, spices, gold, precious gems, brocade, expensive furs, rugs and tapestries were imported and merchants dealing in these goods travelled from as far as Crimea, St. Petersburg, Moscow, the Caucasus, Warsaw, Minsk and Tashkent to participate in the Galician markets. Other foreign traders—Austrians, Germans, Italians, Armenians, Greeks, Turks and Persians—brought silk, copper, coloured glassware, jewellery, exotic foods and clothing which provided further temptation.

A long and traditional part of the protocol between buyer and seller at the market was the bargaining and haggling over a price. There was much to the art of making a deal. When selling an animal or items of clothing, a merchant knew that if he were offered less than half of the asking price, the buyer was not sincere. Flattery and praise would be continually exchanged with each man trying to secure the best price for himself. The etiquette of the transaction dictated that neither party could renege once a deal had been reached.

There were many superstitions associated with a visit to the market and a peasant attentive to the signs would be able to make several predictions. Seeing a bull being led on a tether foretold of his impending participation in a weding party. A dog wearing a muzzle predicted a reward for his temperence. A skinny calf foretold a loss. A fat calf would bring a profit. *Saltseson* (a type of food) meant a visit from an old friend. Underwear—a quarrel with his wife. If he lost a tooth—this foretold a death in the family. Among the Hutsuls, Thursday was considered to be the luckiest day of the week for going to market, especially if taking an animal to sell.

The markets, while immensely popular and always well attended, were infamous for their reputation as places where people wasted their time and were cheated of their money. *Khto bahato yarmarkuie, toi sobi bidu hotuie* (He who spends a lot of time at the market is setting himself up for hardship). The crowds were a haven for thieves and pick-pockets and the people were always warned to be careful. A detachment from the local gendarmerie, however, was usually present to keep the peace and public order.

Zhydachiv

The market in Zhydachiv was held three times a year: January 18, September 10 and November 7.

(above) Selling trousers and vests, Zhydachiv market

(right) Women selling beans and other food-stuffs, Zhydachiv market

(below) A Jewish shop selling sewing materials,
Zhydachiv market

(right) A wheelwright selling wagon wheels,
Zhydachiv market

(below right) Inspecting a pair of boots,
Zhydachiv market

Taking a piglet to market, Zhydachiv

Bolekhiv

The market in Bolekhiv, Dolyna county, was held on January 18, May 6, July 11 and September 26. The weekly market (*torh*) was held every Monday.

(above) On the way home from the market in Bolekhiv

(right) Taking baskets of berries to market, Bolekhiv, Dolyna county

Kosiv

The market in the town of Kosiv was held four times a year: on the Thursday of the first week of Great Lent, the Tuesday before *Voznesennia*, August 25 and October 11. In the event that the appointed day fell on a holiday, the market was held on the following day. The smaller markets (*torhy*) were held every Monday and Friday.

(left) A brass-smith selling rings and bells, Kosiv market

(above) Copper cookwear for sale, Kosiv market

A view of a portion of the market grounds, Kosiv

(above) Armenian-made boots for sale, Kosiv market

(right) A sieve maker, Kosiv market

On their way home from the market in Kosiv

The Denysovy family, Zabolotivtsi, Zhydachiv county

Young village men from Tyshkivtsi, Horodenka county

Villagers

Some of the People CHAPTER 7

In their Sunday best, three families from Rozhniativ, Dolyna county

Townsfolk

(below) Urban residents wearing the newer style of clothing, Bolekhiv, Dolyna county

(right)Townspeople from Strusiv, Terebovlia county

The Hutsuls

The Hutsuls (*Hutsuly*), along with the Boikos and Lemkos, were one of three Ukrainian peoples inhabiting the northern slopes of the Carpathian Mountains. *Hutsulshchyna*, a region of snow-capped mountain peaks, spruce forests and the picturesque valleys of the Cheremosh and Prut Rivers, was the name given to the area in which they lived. It comprised a rather large portion of the Ukrainian ethnographical territory, extending in the west to the settlements of the Boikos and east to Romania.

The Hutsuls, unlike the predominantly agriculturalist Galicians of the plains, made their living primarily by breeding cattle and sheep and working in the forests cutting and transporting timber. The mountainous terrain was not well suited to agriculture and so for them the cultivation of crops was of secondary importance. Corn and potatoes were the principal crops grown, both of which were staples in their diet. Gardening, fruit growing, hunting, fishing and beekeeping were important ancillary activities.

By nature the Hutsuls were very creative and excelled as skillful builders and craftsmen. The area was widely known within Europe for its highly developed domestic handicrafts, especially wood carving, brass work, rug weaving and pottery making, in which the artisans developed their own particular style. In the last decades of the 1800s, trade and craft schools were established in various parts of the region with their products being exported and sold in many of the larger cities of Western Europe.

Owing to the fact that the people lived in scattered settlements and often in isolation, many archaic elements of traditional Hutsul folk culture were preserved. Old rituals were retained as were the folk beliefs, in particular those in the areas of demonology and cosmogony as well as rites and customs relating to the folk calendar. The Hutsuls, in addition to their rich oral tradition of folk music, songs and dances, also developed a unique architectural style and were renowned for their magnificent wooden churches.

Hutsul men going to market, Kosiv

(above) A Hutsul couple at the market in Kosiv

(right) A Hutsul taking some cloth to the market, Kosiv

A Hutsul selecting leather for making shoes, Kosiv market

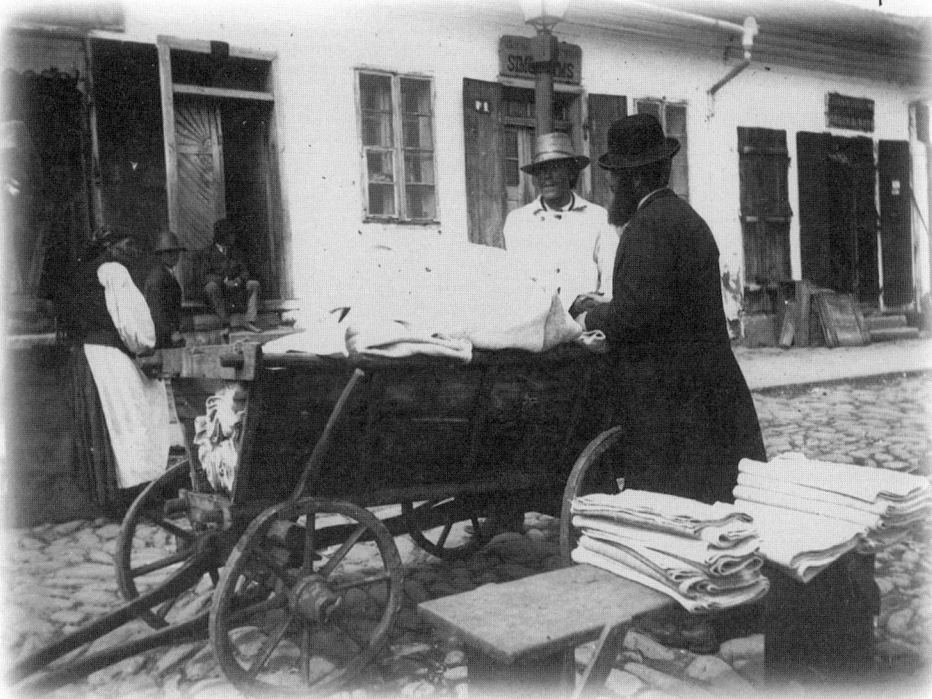

Jews

The Jewish community had a sizable presence in Galicia, especially in the east. In 1890 there were a half million Jews in East Galicia, accounting for 13.5 percent of the population.

Unlike the predominantly peasant Ukrainian and Polish populations, the Jews were mostly townspeople and traders. They occupied a prominent position in Galicia's commercial sector, they were involved in industry and also in the professions. Those living in the rural areas were sometimes engaged in various money-related occupations such as innkeeping, money lending and the leasing and renting of land. In the villages the majority of the Jews were craftsmen and traders and were a popular component at the markets and fairs throughout the region. Many were also employed as tax-collectors and stewards of estates and small industries belonging to the nobility.

The Ukrainians and the Jews in East Galicia lived very different lives from one another. They were separated by differences in dress, speech, diet, religion and occupation. In the small towns the Jews had their own reading halls, libraries, theatre, synagogues and cemeteries—all quite separate from the Christian population—but Jewish children went to the same town and village schools as other children. In some areas, however, private Jewish boys' schools were being built in the 1890s. Though folklore has portrayed them as a rich and powerful force in the countryside, the Jews in the villages and small towns were generally of the same economic stratum as Ukrainian villagers—or poorer—and worked hard to earn a livelihood and support a family.

(above left) A Jewish merchant selling homespun linen at the market in Bolekhiv, Dolyna county

(left) The Jewish tinsmith's shop, Kosiv

A Jewish baker selling buns at the market in Kosiv

Beggars at the Church Feast Day, Liubsha, Zhydachiv county

Beggars

Although at the very bottom of the Galician social and economic ladder, the beggars (*zhebraky*) were not completely undesirable as citizens nor were they entirely neglected. Customarily they were included in the celebrations of holidays and were offered food, especially during the Easter season. They were invited to the commemorative meal held two weeks before *Pylypivka* and took part in the graveside prayers and repast on *Provody*. They gathered at the manor during the Christmas holidays to receive alms from the young men and were especially well represented at the celebrations of a church's feast day where they were given *pyrohy* by the village women. The beggars were also included in the rites and rituals of the funeral and were treated to food and drink by the family of the deceased to thank them for their prayers.

It was a different situation in earlier times. Under Old Poland the beggars in Galicia were subjected to harsh treatment by the authorities and suffered greatly at the hand of the village reeve. They were often whipped, beaten or even sentenced to death by hanging, actions which were justified by the officials who claimed that the beggars caused the spread of disease and epidemic. The beggars carried sticks with burrs or sharp pieces of metal attached to the end as a means of protection from dogs or other animals. St. Mykolai, the patron saint of the beggars and care-giver to all unfortunate ones, was believed to keep them safe from harm.

In Galicia it was common to find two types of beggars within the community. There were society's legitimate poor, the handicapped, orphans and other citizens whose existence depended on begging as a result of their individual circumstances. They were typically seen in the village handing out small bunches of herbs, offering prayers or singing to the accompaniment of their *lira* while gratefully acknowledging every offering of money, bread or groats. Working alongside them were the so-called professional beggars. These were imposters who made for themselves a thriving business by posing as beggars. They travelled the countryside in groups and used a secret sign language among themselves. The drawing of the face of a cat scratched in the dirt in front of a house informed the other "beggars" that a sympathetic woman lived inside and would be likely to offer them her charity.

The beggars performed other roles within the community in addition to offering their prayers. A beggar woman (*zhebrachka*) was usually called upon to wash and dress the body of a deceased family member for burial. The beggars were included and participated in the ritual of the *posydinnia* during the time in which the body was lying inside the house. Some of the more able bodied beggars were responsible for sweeping and washing the church floor for which they were paid a small remuneration or given donations of food.

A large role in the beggar's life was the singing of his special songs (*zhebratski pisni*). Many were religious in nature and were sung during funerals or feasts commemorating the dead. Others were more apocalyptic with references to the judgement day and the end of the world, or were sung as laments about the cruelty and injustices of society, past dreams and lost opportunities. The songs would be sung in a monotone fashion with the verses repeated over and over as the beggars attempted to procure the charity and good will of others.

Village schoolhouse, older style, Humeniv, Kalush county

Schools

In its construction, the schoolhouse was identical to that of the village house. It was made of logs, plastered with clay, with a thatched roof and a floor made of packed clay. Schools in more affluent areas were likely to have shingled rooves, large windows and a wooden floor. The floor plans were standard for the whole Austrian Empire, and frequently included a teacher's residence within its walls. The most characteristic feature of the schoolhouse was the bell tower or belfry set atop the building itself. The building of the schoolhouses was the responsibility of the individual village or town but occasionally there would be a subsidy from county or Galician authorities or donations from the local manor or the Austrian Emperor.

Compulsory schooling for children of ages 6 to 12 was established by Austrian law in 1869 but only gradually implemented in Galicia. The village school was to impart a basic education to the citizenry. Language arts (reading and writing), arithmetic, religion and singing formed the core of the curriculum in grades 1 and 2. A second language (one of the official languages of the Austrian Empire) was added in grade 2. In grades 3 and 4 children were introduced to natural sciences, geography, history, drawing, geometry, and domestic science for girls and physical education for boys. Besides the basic curriculum a growing number of courses were offered in technical and vocational subjects such as horticulture, beekeeping and agriculture. Many schools had their own vegetable gardens, orchards and even functioning apiaries which were used for instructional purposes. Many schools had small libraries by 1890. Field trips to museums, factories or sight-seeing in the cities supplemented the basic curriculum.

Children in the rural areas of East Galicia attended school for a half day only: the older ones in the morning from 7:00 am and the younger ones in the afternoons to 6:00 pm. The length of the school year varied but was generally 46 weeks. There was no school on Sundays or Thursday afternoons and all Catholic holy days, both of Latin and Eastern rites, were school holidays.

The village school was taught by one or two teachers depending on the number of pupils. The regulations stated that if the number of children in a school exceeded 80, there were to be two teachers; three if the number exceeded 160. In the Ukrainian areas the primary language of instruction was to be Ukrainian, but because of the Polish domination of the Galician School Council Polish was often the language in which Ukrainian children were taught.

During the nineteenth century there was a steady increase in the number of village schools in the region. Between 1869–81, the number of elementary schools in Galicia rose from 2,476 to 2,925. Most of the newly established schools were one-teacher schools. Between 1883–91, a further 1,224 schools were organized, bringing the total for Galicia to 4,149, among them many larger multi-teacher schools.

The Built Landscape CHAPTER 8

(below) A modern style village schoolhouse, Turady, Zhydachiv county

Masonry Ukrainian church, Liubsha, Zhydachiv county

Churches

The church was an integral part of the lives of the people and one to which they held extremely strong attachments. It served them not only in their religious and spiritual needs but also as the centre of their cultural, social and, until the increase in the number of schools, educational activities. Belonging to the church was the main indicator of the reputation of a villager and his regular attendance was a sign to all of his integrity and respectability.

As the place of worship for the village's Christian congregation, the church was the place for the celebration of the Sunday Sabbath and other holy days, the baptism of children, the performance of the marriage ceremony and certain funeral rites and rituals. It was also an often sought refuge for prayer and comfort during times of illness, a death in the family or other domestic problems. Village processions, such as those marking the anniversary of the 1848 abolition of compulsory labour (May 3) or the beginning of the harvest, were usually organized and led from the church. It was the site for the celebration of the parish's saint's day—one of the community's most loved events—and the usual starting point for carollers during the Christmas holidays.

As the main focal point in the village, the church cast an imposing presence. It was set typically in the centre of the settlement together with the other parish buildings, the parsonage, bell tower and often the cemetery. In East Galicia there was a great diversity in church styles with each region having developed its own characteristic architecture. The mountain regions were known for their rich tradition of wooden sacral architecture while in the villages of the Galician plains stone churches gained favour and became increasingly popular during the eighteenth and nineteenth centuries. In the last decades of the 1800s, as the affluence and self-worth of the peasants continued to grow, there was much construction of churches, both completely new ones and new structures to replace the old.

Wooden Ukrainian church and bell tower, Izydorivka, Zhydachiv county

Roadside Crosses and Chapels

The custom of setting by roadsides tall wooden crosses and chapels existed as early as the Middle Ages. They were found in or near virtually every village, town and city in Galicia and exhibited a great variety in form and richness of detail. The structures were typically built from wood—oak was often the preferred building material because its considerable hardness was resistant to weathering—although the use of stone was equally widespread.

The crosses and chapels served a variety of functions. They were set at intersections of roads, on routes leading to hospitals or in front of churches as symbols of divine protection. They were erected at crossroads, long considered to be dangerous places, to provide protection from restless spirits. Erected on the sites of former battles, in front of cemeteries and within them and at crime scenes, they were believed to contribute to the salvation of the dead and to protect the living from harm. A popular practise was to place them at the entrance or in the main square of a village or town to keep the residents safe. On a more practical level they functioned as landmarks for travellers or as a place for prayer during a work day.

Numerous roadside crosses and chapels in East Galicia were built in honour of particular saints who were believed to grant favours or perform special services. St. Panteleimon safeguarded the people from sickness, St. Bonyfatii was believed to keep them from drinking and St. Mykolai protected people from drowning. In earlier times the crosses and chapels served as a place for public events. Thieves were whipped in front of them, young women could be punished there for alleged promiscuity, and they served as backdrops for hangings or executions. Folklore tells of numerous chapels which were haunted. On the other hand the building of a chapel could be seen to be a means of driving away evil spirits that were believed to inhabit certain locations.

The crosses and chapels figured prominently in the lives of the people. Processions of villagers led by the priest would gather at the cross in order to bless the crops or mark the beginning of the harvest. Many were erected as signs of gratitude to God and to the Emperor Ferdinand for the abolition of compulsory labour in 1848 and served as the sites for the festive anniversary celebrations. An item of clothing belonging to a sick person hung on a cross or chapel was believed to cure the illness. Anyone who passed by the same roadside cross nine times in the same day while glancing at the top would immediately be visited by the Devil who would ask *Choho potrebuiesh?* ("What do you need?") Any favour could then be granted but would come at the price of the person's soul.

Carved wooden roadside cross, Tsutsylivtsi, Zhydachiv county

Roadside chapel, Tyshkivtsi, Horodenka county

Workmen taking a break while doing road repairs, Strusiv, Terebovlia county

Road Building

The best roads in Galicia were the imperial highways (*kraievi dorohy*). These were built and largely maintained by the Austrian government using a British system of road construction known as macadamization. Roads of a lower quality were the provincial and the county roads (*povitovi dorohy*). Although these roadways were supposed to be built on the same principles, though not as wide, the latter in particular were generally in poor condition and badly neglected. At the bottom of the scale were the field roads which connected outlying parts of a settlement with the main village.

Many new roads were built during the last decades of the 1800s and added greatly to the region's expanding network of transportation systems. Construction costs were generally borne by the state, the Land or the county, and in 1899 the Austrian parliament allocated 460,000 *gulden* toward the building of new county roads in Galicia. The construction and maintenance of the roadways was assisted by the villagers from whom contributions of both work and materials, *sharvarok*, were required by law. Compulsory roadwork could amount to as much as six days per year for each Galician landowner, but this was lowered in 1884 and reduced to two days per year in 1896. The peasants resented this imposition because although the large landowners used the roads most, it was they who had to maintain them.

Even the best constructed Galician road had its problems. Mud was a great hazard on county roads, particularly after spring and fall rains, and they were dusty in summer. The military was to blame for the poor condition of many roads and during times of heavy manoeuvres they would be left rutted or otherwise damaged. Steep gradients made for other difficulties in transportation, especially in the mountain regions. These problems notwithstanding, the Galician roads were used and well-travelled by the people, bringing the villagers into closer contact with each other and with more distant towns and cities.

Making crushed rock, Horodenka

A village procession on the anniversary of the abolition of compulsory labour, Zabolotivtsi, Zhydachiv county

Placing a wreath on the cross of freedom on May 3, 1892 in commemoration of the anniversary of the abolition of compulsory labour in 1848, Zabolotivtsi, Zhydachiv county

1848 Remembered

The observance of the May 3 anniversary of the abolition of compulsory labour in the Austrian Empire in 1848 was a great national holiday. Festivities were held throughout the whole Monarchy with citizens from each of the crownlands ceremoniously marking the day and celebrating the freedoms which it brought. It was a time for remembrance, thankfulness and being mindful of the past.

The anniversary celebrations typically began with a service at the church. This was followed by the villagers walking in procession to the Cross of Freedom, often to the accompaniment of music or singing and carrying colourful flags and church banners. A programme of events would be planned at the site. Prayers were said for the Emperor Ferdinand in whose name the emancipation of the peasantry had been decreed, and for those who toiled and died under serfdom. The village women would serve a

Special Days CHAPTER 9

community meal, the church choir performed and there were likely to be recitations or readings from literary works. A special part of the events was the honouring of village elders who worked under serfdom. Music and dancing concluded the celebrations. It was not uncommon for these festivities to be attended by hundreds or even thousands of people.

Many times outdoor public assemblies (*viche*) would be organized to coincide with the events of the day. Speeches, debates or lectures on any one of a number of topics of local and national interest were held following the commemorative festivities. They were delivered by visiting dignitaries, prominent political or religious figures or by the villagers and townsfolk themselves. These meetings were held on site or moved to locations such as the reading hall, schoolhouse or National Home. An impression of the events and of the significance of the day is given in the following excerpt from a report in *Svoboda* on the 1898 anniversary celebration in the town of Husiatyn, on Galicia's border with the Russian Empire:

Whoever missed Husiatyn's Fiftieth Anniversary celebrations of the abolition of compulsory labour will forever be sorry. This was an event the

Corpus Christi, girls carrying the processional icon, Berezhnytsia Korolivska, Zhydachiv county

likes of which has never been seen before. There were so many people! Young men on horseback with their animals immaculately groomed, the townspeople each dressed in their festive clothing…everyone had come to take part in the procession.

At the church the people listened attentively to the words of the priest and offered their thanks to God. After the service they marched in procession to the cross which was decorated with banners and icons. Everyone walked around it three times and then took their positions to the side, their heads bowed as the priests said prayers for Emperor Ferdinand.

In the afternoon fireworks called the people to an outdoor assembly where speeches about the era of compulsory labour were given. Everything was orderly, beautiful and festive!

Corpus Christi

One of Galicia's favourite special days was Corpus Christi. Established as a general festival of the Roman Catholic Church in 1264, its original celebration on the ninth Thursday after Easter was transferred to the first Sunday following the Feast of the Trinity where it remained fixed. It began to be celebrated as a religious festival for Ukrainians in Galicia in 1891.

A central part of the festivities surrounding Corpus Christi (*Bozhe tilo*), literally "Body of Christ," was the public procession. The people believed that whoever did not participate in this event would fail to live out the year and so with little exception they were attended by everyone. The procession was led through the village by the priest and members of the church brotherhood. They carried the Gospel, crosses, lighted candles and the monstrance containing the Host to an altar adorned with branches of poplar, linden, birch and plaited wreaths assembled outside in the church yard or cemetery. The ceremony which followed consisted of special prayers and religious songs and culminated at the altar with the priest raising the Host toward heaven and making with it the sign of the cross to the four corners of the world before the kneeling faithful.

The wreaths which were used to decorate the altar were made by the village women on the eve of Corpus Christi. They were plaited from sprigs of mint, thyme, basil, periwinkle and marigold flowers and were blessed by the priest on the day of the celebration. The wreaths were collected following the holiday and saved by the women who used them throughout the year in

Corpus Christi, a group of girls in procession, Berezhnytsia Korolivska, Zhydachiv county

Corpus Christi, the faithful listening to a sermon by the church, Berezhnytsia Korolivska, Zhydachiv county

various folk medicine practises. The people believed that the herbs and plants would possess their healing and curative powers only if they had been accorded these ritual blessings. One of the wreaths would be hung on the wall above the door inside the house or in the stable as a means of keeping away evil spirits. Another would be crushed with the hands and added to the feed for the cattle in order to keep them healthy.

During the week following Corpus Christi the people would come to the church and collect the branches which had been used to decorate the altar. They were taken home and thrust upright in the barley field and cabbage patch in order to keep the ravens from doing any damage. One of the branches would be stuck into the grain field before sunrise on the first Friday after Corpus Christi as a means of protecting the crop from disease and guaranteeing a bountiful harvest.

Obzhynky

From ancient times Ukrainians have celebrated festively the end of the harvest. In East Galicia many of the harvesting tasks were traditionally considered to be women's work and so its ceremonious beginning, *zazhynky*, the rites and rituals of the completion of the harvest, *obzhynky*, and the singing of the special harvest songs were performed mainly by women.

The harvest generally began in mid summer about a week after the feast of St. Peter (*sviatyi Petro*) on June 29. The first of the harvest rituals was *zazhynky*, the ritual cutting and binding of the first sheaf of grain for which there was particular reverence as a symbol of the harvest and harbinger of the crop for the following year. The sheaf was kept and threshed separately from the rest and its grain blessed in church and mixed with the seed grain for the fall planting.

Obzhynky (also *dozhynky*), the celebration of the end of the harvest and the bringing in of the grain from the fields, was the most ceremonious of the rituals. As the work neared completion, the reapers made the *Spasova boroda* (Saviour's Beard) or simply *Boroda* (Beard), a bound but uncut sheaf of grain with the ears turned toward the ground. The grain from the *Boroda* was shelled from the ears and sown among the roots while young boys or unmarried men crawled through the stalks to insure the bounty of the following harvest. At the same time the women tossed their sickles behind them over their shoulders. The next year would see a good crop if they landed with the blades sticking in the soil.

Using stalks of grain gathered from each of the harvested sheaves on the field the women plaited an elaborate wreath which they decorated with flowers and coloured ribbons. This was ceremoniously placed on the head of one of the reapers, their *kniahynia* (princess), who would be led in procession to the lord or master on whose field they were harvesting. In some areas it was also a custom to make a flower (*kvitka*) which consisted of five or six smaller sheaves bound together in a shape resembling a large flower. This ritual, as with all of the rituals of the *Obzhynky* celebration, was performed to the singing of special harvest songs.

When they arrived on the yard the women called out in song for the lord to come and greet them. He would appear with the traditional offerings of bread and salt and then accept the wreath from the *kniahynia*. She bowed before him three times in succession while extending blessings of health and prosperity. "May God grant you the means to sow and plough again next year and may He keep us healthy so we may harvest for you." His reply called for the safekeeping and happiness of them all. "May God grant that we live in good health and that the future holds for you a happy married life." Following the blessings everyone was invited inside for a celebration with music and dancing and to partake of the food and drink which had been prepared especially for this occasion.

Obzhynky being celebrated at the completion of the harvest, the reapers extend wishes of prosperity to the landlord, Zbora, Kalush county

A group of men sitting around the bonfire, Denysiv, Ternopil county

The Great Day

Khrystos voskres! Voistynu voskres! ("Christ is Risen! He is truly Risen!") These words of the traditional Easter greeting echoed throughout the towns and villages of East Galicia in joyful celebration of this greatest of days. Easter (*Velykden*, literally the "Great Day") was the most important of religious festivals for Ukrainians, its pagan origins long since adapted to the traditions of the Christian church. It was a time of happiness, cheerful rejoice and one filled with the hope and renewal of this holy day with the entire community coming together in common celebration.

Preparations for Easter began with the preceding forty day Lenten season and the rites and rituals of the Holy Week starting with the blessing of the willow boughs in church on Palm Sunday. The people prepared themselves spiritually through fasting, prayer and penitence, and attended to the physical surroundings of their home environment in eager and anxious anticipation of the celebration of Christ's Resurrection. Houses were cleaned, repaired and whitewashed, and the yards tidied and set in order. Peas, beans and the spring crops were planted in the belief that they would grow abundantly if sown during this week. The work was done in earnest in an effort to complete the preparations before *Strasnyi chetver* (Holy Thursday) after which any kind of heavy work was forbidden.

Good Friday (*Velyka piatnytsia*), the day of the solemn commemoration of Christ's crucifixtion, was marked with the silencing of the church bells. The bells—rung on occasions throughout the preceding period—were silenced with wooden clappers and not rung again until Easter Sunday. No work would be done on this day and it was considered a great sin to chop wood, hew anything with an axe, or sing. The women typically baked the *paska* and planted cabbage on Good Friday. At the church service on this day the Holy Shroud (*plashchanytsia*) was carried solemnly around the church three times and then placed in a symbolic grave inside.

The preparatory activities continued on Holy Saturday. The faithful maintained their routine of fasting and prayer, the Easter foods were prepared and cooked, and women and girls decorated the ritual *pysanky*. It was a custom for the young men of the village to build a large bonfire on this day. It was made in a clearing or within the churchyard but always in such a location that it would be seen by the whole village. They recited a special prayer as it was lit and jumped through the flames or surrounded themselves in the smoke in order to benefit from the cleansing and purifying powers which the fire was believed to possess.

Easter Sunday, the Great Day, began with the Easter matins and the celebration of high mass at the church during which the Easter foods were blessed. Tradition dictated that none of the food could be eaten until it was blessed by the priest. The women prepared and brought baskets containing *paska*, cheese, eggs (*krashanky and pysanky*), salt, horseradish, pork, butter, lard (*salo*), spring onions and sausage. After the blessing the food was taken home and each of the farm buildings visited before going into the house and breaking the fast. Some of the salt was sprinkled beside each of the entrances as a deterent for evil spirits, and a piece of *paska* was cut from the loaf, dipped in salt or honey and fed to each of the animals.

Following the meal the people gathered at the churchyard or cemetery for the performance of the *hayivky* and the Easter games. The church bells were rung all day long by the young men of the village. Whoever rang the bells on Easter Sunday would be blessed with a good harvest, especially of buckwheat, and so the men often engaged with one another in friendly competition for their turn at the ropes. The festivities continued until nightfall and resumed the following day on Easter Monday.

Young men ringing the bells,
Denysiv, Ternopil county

EASTER CHAPTER 10

Villagers at the Easter matins awaiting the blessing of the food, Denysiv, Ternopil county

hayivky

Kryvyi Tanets ("The Crooked Dance"). *Perepilka* ("The Quail"). *Ohirochky* ("Cucumbers"). *Vorotar* ("The Gatekeeper"). These were only a few of the names of the popular and much loved *hayivky* or ritual spring song-dances which were an integral part of the celebrations. It was impossible to imagine an Easter without them. Their performance, once vital as a means of driving away winter, calling forth spring and imparting new life to the surrounding environment, was now merely symbolic but still deeply entrenched in the celebration of the season.

The name *hayivky* (sing. *hayivka*; also *hahilky*, *yahivky* and *yahilky* among other variations) is of ancient origin and dates, perhaps, to pre-Christian times when the songs and dances were performed in groves (*hayi*) as a part of the pagan spring rituals of invocation. They came to be separated from their original seasonal adaptation and were connected to the church calendar as a part of the Easter celebrations. The advent of Christianity and the growing influence of the Church brought about a dualism or "double faith" which was characteristic of many Ukrainian rituals—and indeed of those of other peoples—and which was sustained well into the modern era.

The *hayivky* were combinations of songs, dances and dramatized games, often in the form of a dialogue between two groups of singers and dancers. The lyrics were characteristically short and simple. The song was of secondary importance to the rhythm and movement of the performers whose original primary objective was to generate and transfer to their surroundings the energy needed to bring forth the new season and invoke a bountiful harvest. Other prominent themes in the *hayivky* were related to the beginning of the agricultural cycle and the courtship and marriage season.

Participants in the *hayivky* were almost exclusively young unmarried women; the exception to the rule were those who were recently wed. Married women and widows took part only as spectators. Further reflecting the rite of ancestor worship during the Easter season was their performance near the church or within the cemetery. *Zhuchok* ("Little Beetle") was one of the most popular *hayivky*. The women would group themselves in pairs, join hands which they crossed at the wrist, and stand abreast in a long line. A young girl, the *zhuchok*, then climbed on top of the womens' arms and walked along this "bridge," steadying herself with her hands on the shoulders of the women, while the lyrics were sung. The pairs of women over whose arms the *zhuchok* had crossed would then leave their position and move to the end of the line as the *hayivka* continued.

The *hayivka Ptashok* ("Little Bird") being performed on the church yard during the Easter celebrations, Voltsniv, Zhydachiv county

Hayivka Moloda ("The Young Lady"), Denysiv, Ternopil county

(left) *Hayivka* being performed by the church, Liubsha, Zhydachiv county

(below left) *Khodyt zhuchok po zhuchyni,/A zhuchykha po derevyni./Hrai, zhuchku, hrai! Hayivka Zhuchok* ("The Little Beetle"), Denysiv, Ternopil county

(below) *Hayivka Zelman,* Denysiv, Ternopil county

A group of young boys playing the game *Tserkovtsia* ("Little Church"), Voltsniv, Zhydachiv county

Easter Games

The Easter games, played alongside the *hayivky*, were another characteristic part of the celebrations. They were performed during the first three days of Easter, continued on *Provody* and again later in the year on *Zeleni sviata*. The games were the domain of the young men and boys who delighted and amused the crowd of onlookers by demonstrating their prowess and athletic skills in a wide variety of activities, usually running, jumping, leaping or other displays of energy. At the same time another group of men would be ringing the church bells or collecting and trading *pysanky* from the village's most marriageable young women.

One of the most popular Easter games was *Tserkovtsia* ("Little Church") in which a group of four or six young men would stand in a circle, each embracing one another with their arms interlocked around their waists. Another two or three would climb up and position themselves on top of their shoulders and then the group would walk around the church while maintaining this position. The successful performance of this game was testimony to the strength and acrobatic skills of the participants.

Another favourite was *Vil* ("The Ox"). It was performed as one of the men, holding a whip, led the rest of the participants holding hands and forming a long line behind him, in a game of follow-the-leader. The line moved in different formations around the churchyard or through the cemetery and anyone not following quickly or skillfully enough would have the whip cracked in his direction. The line typically contained as many as 20 or 30 participants. Popular too were *Pereskachky* ("Leapfrog"), *Tsisar* ("The Emperor") and *Viyna* ("War").

Young men performing *Tserkovtsia*, Tyshkivtsi, Horodenka county

Young men performing the game *Vil* ("The Ox"), Denysiv, Ternopil county

Chy ye myshi v stozi? ("Are There Mice in the Haystack?")
being performed near Zhydachiv

Young boys playing the game *byrky* with carved sticks of wood, Denysiv, Ternopil county

Drenched Monday

Easter Monday in East Galicia, called *Oblyvanyi ponedilok* (literally "Drenched Monday"), was a day for the playful ritual drenching or splashing with water of young women by their male peers. Among Ukrainians the act of splashing during the Easter season was an adaptation of an ancient pagan custom of invoking luck, health and marital happiness and regarded by some as a symbolic means of calling for rain. It was known among other European peoples and probably came to Galicia from Western Europe.

The splashing, *oblyvannia*, was practised by villagers, townspeople and members of the gentry alike and with great abandon. No woman was safe as the men hid behind fences, in barns or on top of rooves with pots and pails of water as they waited to splash the unsuspecting women. Some of the men were more efficient in their technique and simply picked them up, carried them to the river and tossed them directly in the water. One of the greatest delights was splashing women found still sleeping in their beds and keeping dry was a futile effort for any woman who overslept. Cautious villagers were known to remove bed covers, rugs and pillows in advance of the pails of water which were dumped through many windows on Drenched Monday.

Customarily the women would attempt to appease the men and curb the splashing by offering them a *pysanka* or *krashanka* which they had decorated themselves. Hutsul women did not hand over the offering directly but engaged with the men in a friendly struggle before surrendering the gift. The splashing games stopped during the church service but were resumed afterwards at the cemetery and lasted until vespers that evening. In some areas the custom was reversed on the day after Drenched Monday when the women had the unrestricted right to splash the men.

In some regions of *Hutsulshchyna* Easter Monday was called *volochivnyi* or *volochilnyi ponedilok*. On this day the young men would "wander around" (*volochatsia*) and visit the women in search of *pysanky*. This was also a time for them to investigate their matchmaking prospects, and evening parties would be held where the young people gathered. Children would take *pyrohy* to their grandparents or godparents on this day and in return were given a small gift or some coins.

Splashing the girls on Easter Monday, Demenka Lisova, Zhydachiv county

A Time to Remember

Ancestor worship and the rite of commemoration, a theme found throughout the whole of the Easter season, was observed most ceremoniously on *Provody*, the first Sunday after Easter, with special prayers and a graveside meal. It was believed that God allowed the spirits to return to Earth four times during the year—on Christmas Eve (*Sviat vechir*), the Feast of the Trinity (*Zeleni sviata*), the Feast of the Transfiguration of the Lord (*Spasa*) and during Easter on Holy Thursday when they stayed until *Provody*.

Provody, the name literally meaning "sending off" or "seeing off," was a day of solemn commemoration. The ritual often began with a procession, led by the clergy and the choir, and with the villagers carrying banners, crosses, candles and holy pictures, to the cemetery grounds. There the priest performed a *parastas*, a special service for the dead, and at the request of a family member would say a *panakhyda* (prayers for the dead) afterward at individual grave sites.

The graveside meal, a central part of the commemorative ritual, consisted of a selection of the remaining Easter foods and followed the prayers. The men and women, at the graves of their parents or other family members, would crack a *krashanka* on the cross and then give it to the beggars or the village poor who were invited to participate. The remainder of the blessed Easter food, salt and some liquor was left at the grave saying *Yizhte, pyite i nas spomynaite* ("Eat, drink and remember us"). These offerings, like the performance of the *hayivky* and the Easter games, were remnants of practices of pre-Christian origin intended to honour and placate the spirits in order that they would provide the family with a bountiful harvest.

In some regions of East Galicia *Provody* was celebrated on the first Monday or on the third day after Easter. In all cases the performance of this ritual was carried out exclusively by women with the men and young people of both genders typically not taking an active part. Their main role in this commemorative feast was perhaps an indication of its origins during the matriarchal period of Ukrainian history. Before the celebration the women would decorate the graves and crosses with the herb *tatarske zillia* (Sweet Flag), a custom which dated from earliest times.

Provody. Villagers offering prayers for the dead (*panakhyda*), Voltsniv, Zhydachiv county

Provody, Denysiv, Ternopil county

Panakhyda and giving the beggars food, *Provody*, Denysiv, Ternopil county

Funeral procession, Tyshkivtsi, Horodenka county

Funerals

The entire proceedings of the funeral *(pokhoron)* were observed and attended to carefully by Ukrainians. Death was long regarded in folk belief as an act of transference from this world to that of the after-life and one which was made easier by the performance of the prescribed rites and rituals of the funeral—the mournful sounding of the *trembita* among the Hutsuls. The coffin shrouded in black, followed by family members, friends and carried in solemn procession to the church and cemetery. The graveside prayers and those recited on the days following the burial. The execution of each of the rites was a required part in the making of this transition. It marked the end of one life but the beginning of another.

Funerals typically took place three days after death. The body was washed and dressed in preparation for the funeral, a task sometimes delegated to a village beggar woman. Men and women were dressed in their festive clothing for burial. Young children and unmarried men and women of any age would be dressed in traditional wedding attire. Custom dictated that the body was never to be left unattended during the time it was kept inside the house. Family members and friends would participate in the *posydinnia*, the ritual sitting with the deceased, to pray and sing songs as a means of protecting the body from the intervention of evil spirits.

The coffin was carried out of the house feet first and knocked three times at the threshold of each room on the day of the funeral so that the deceased could bid farewell to the house. The last person to leave would close the door as quickly as possible as a symbolic means of preventing another death. In some regions the coffin would be strewn with the grain threshed from the Christmas *didukh*.

Sleighs, horse-drawn wagons, or the sturdy arms and shoulders of some of the mourners, were used to transport the coffin to the church and cemetery. Mares were never used in the funeral procession because it was believed they would be rendered barren if they took part. The coffin was sealed so that the deceased would not leave and lowered into the ground with the head pointing west following the services at the cemetery. The grave was dug deeply and sprinkled with poppy seeds so that the deceased would not walk after death. Each grave was marked with a cross made from wood or stone depending on regional custom and the wealth of the individual family.

The people returned to the home of the deceased for a funeral meal *(tryzna)* following the burial. A required part of this repast was a ritual dish of cooked wheat or barley grains and honey called *kolyvo*. Those who carried the coffin or dug the grave would first wash their hands and then touch them to the stove in a special cleansing ritual before eating. The offering of food after the funeral was a custom of ancient origin and one which expressed the family's gratitude to the people for their prayers for the soul of the deceased.

Food and drink were left at the grave for the deceased in the days following the funeral. Bread, fruit, the remaining *kolyvo*, and jars of water were set out on the windowsills of the house. The traditional belief was that the soul remained close to home until the completion of the last of the funeral rites before leaving for the other world on the fortieth day after death. Special graveside prayers for the dead were said on this day (similar prayers were said on the third and ninth days after death), on the first anniversary, and every year thereafter.

To the Other World CHAPTER 11

A village funeral, taking the coffin off the wagon in front of the church, Tyshkivtsi, Horodenka county

A village funeral, prayers beside the coffin, Tyshkivtsi, Horodenka county

Cemeteries

The village cemetery *(kladovyshche, also tsvyntar)* was neither a place feared nor avoided by the people. Located near the church, its grounds sanctified in the belief in the eternal life of the spirit after death, it was a place of peace, prayer, reflection and commemoration. The villagers gathered communally several times during the year for graveside prayers and services, especially during the Easter season, and by themselves or as families to observe the anniversaries of deaths. Women bringing offerings of bread to the cemetery for the *parastas* took it fresh from the oven because the steam rising from the loaves was believed to ascend directly to heaven and take with it their special prayers. The graves of unmarried men and women were decorated with cranberry branches on All Saints Day and those of their married counterparts with juniper boughs.

The individual graves were covered with small mounds of earth, low ones among the Boikos and the Hutsuls but up to a half metre in height in other regions of East Galicia, and marked with wooden or stone crosses of various shapes and sizes. The Boikos of Stryi and Sambir counties usually erected small, wooden crosses and placed clay pots on the graves as a symbolic means of leaving water for the deceased. The Galicians of the plains characteristically built crosses which were very tall. They were simple in form with their only ornamentation being a small, protective wooden roof or decorative fretwork added to the ends of the crossbar. The Hutsuls exhibited the greatest artistry and originality in the design and ornamentation of their grave markers. Crosses made from stone were erected in some regions and appeared with varying degrees of frequency.

In earlier times, with the belief that the spirits of deceased family members became the guardians or protectors of the family, there existed the custom of burying bodies near the house, especially under the floor or beneath the threshold which then became sacred spaces within the dwelling. There was also a time when people were buried at a crossroads. These locations have long been regarded as unsafe because of restless souls unable to pass on to the afterlife.

Cemeteries in East Galicia, unlike the farm yards, were rarely fenced. Their boundaries were defined, rather, by deep ditches. Wild flowers growing in a cemetery were said to have been sown by God's own hand. During times of epidemics, communities would allocate space for separate burial grounds, such as those for cholera victims which were found in many villages, in an attempt to prevent the spread of disease.

Tombstone of a villager who died in 1888, Hnizdychiv, Zhydachiv county

103

(above) A village cemetery with tall wooden crosses,
Zabolotivtsi, Zhydachiv county

(above right) The old cholera cemetery, Tyshkivtsi, Horodenka county

(right) A village cemetery, Tyshkivtsi, Horodenka county

Decorated crosses in the village cemetery, Strusiv, Terebovlia county

Sources Consulted

Batkivshchyna, Lviv, 1886, 1887, 1888, 1890, 1891, 1895, 1896

Bujak, Franciszek. *Galicya*, 2 vols., Lviv, 1908–10

Deia, O.I., ed. *Ihry ta pisni vesniano-litnia poeziia trudovoho roku*, Kiev, 1963

Dobrowolski, Kazimierz et al., eds. *Etnografia Polska XII*, Wrocław, 1968

Fryś-Pietraszkowa, Ewa et al. *Sztuka Ludowa w Polsce*, Warsaw, 1988

Gemeindelexikon der im Reichsrate vertretenen Königreiche und Länder, Bearbeitet auf Grund der Ergebnisse der Volkszahlung vom 31. Dezember 1900, Galizien. Vienna, 1907

Geography of Ukraine, n.p., Doncaster, Australia, 1985

Gospodarz Wiejski, Lviv, 1890

Hatfield, Audrey Wynne. *Pleasures of Wild Plants*, New York, 1966

Himka, John-Paul. *Galician Villagers and the Ukrainian National Movement in the Nineteenth Century*, New York, 1988

Hoshko, Yu. et al., ed. *Hutsulshchyna*, Kiev, 1987

Hryniuk, Stella. *Peasants with Promise: Ukrainians in Southeastern Galicia 1880–1900*, Edmonton, 1991

Hurzhii, I.O. *Ukraiina v systemi vse-rosiiskoho rynku 60–90 rokiv XIX st.*, Kiev, 1968

Inglot, Stefan et al., eds. *Historia Chłopów Polskich*, vol. 2, Warsaw, 1972

Kaliendar Misionar, Lviv, 1913

Kolberg, Oskar. *Chełmskie I* in *Dzieła Wszystkie*, vol. 33, Warsaw, 1964

Ibid., *Chełmskie II* in *Dzieła Wszystkie*, vol. 34, Warsaw, 1964

Ibid., *Krakowskie I* in *Dzieła Wszystkie*, vol. 5, Wrocław, 1962

Ibid., *Lubelskie II* in *Dzieła Wszystkie*, vol. 17, Krakow, 1962

Ibid., *Pokucie I* in *Dzieła Wszystkie*, vol. 29, Wrocław, 1962

Ibid., *Przemyskie* in *Dzieła Wszystkie*, vol. 35, Krakow, 1964

Ibid., *RuśCzerwona I* in *Dzieła Wszystkie*, vol. 56, Wrocław, 1976

Ibid., *Ruś Karpacka I* in *Dzieła Wszystkie*, vol. 54, Wrocław, 1970

Koropeckyj, I.S., ed. *Ukrainian Economic History: Interpretative Essays*, Cambridge, Mass., 1991

Kosmina, Tamara. *Silske zhytlo Podillia kinets XIX – XX st.*, Kiev, 1980

Krzysztofowicz, Stefania. *O Sztuce Ludowej w Polsce*, Warsaw, 1972

Kubijovych, Volodymyr, ed. *Ukraine: A Concise Encyclopedia*, 2 vols., Toronto, 1963, 1973

Kylymnyk, Stepan. *Ukrayinskyi rik u narodnykh zvychaiakh v istorychnomu osvitlenni*, Winnipeg-Toronto, 1962

Metropolitan Ilarion. *Dokhrystiianski viruvannia ukraiinskoho narodu*, Winnipeg, 1965

Moszyński, *Kazimierz. Kultura Ludowa Słowian*, vol. I, Kraków, 1929; vol. II, Kraków, 1934

Plaviuk, *Volodymyr. Prypovidky abo ukraiinska narodnia filosofiia*, Edmonton, 1946

Potichnyj, Peter and Howard Aster, eds. *Ukrainian-Jewish Relations in Historical Perspective*, Edmonton, 1990

Pysmo z Prosvity, Lviv, 1878

Rotoff, *Basil et al. Monuments to Faith*, Winnipeg, 1990

Sirka, A., *The Nationality Question in Austrian Education: The Case of the Ukrainians in Galicia*, Frankfurt, 1980

Světozor, Praha, 1890

Svoboda, Lviv, 1897, 1899

Szczypka, Jozef. *Kalendarz Polski*, Warsaw, 1979

Szuchiewicz, Włodzimierz. *Huculszczyzna*, vol. I, Lviv, 1902; vol. II, Lviv, 1902; vol. III, Lviv, 1904

Voropai, Oleksa. *Zvychaii nashoho narodu, Etnohrafichnyi narys*, 2 vols., Munich, 1958 and 1966

Vovk, Fedir. *Studiyi z ukrayinskoii etnohrafiyi ta antropolohiii*, New York, 1976

Zlatá Praha, Praha, 1887

Glossary of Ukrainian Words

Blahovishchennia: The Feast of the Annunciation, the traditional beginning of the spring period.

didukh: A sheaf of grain, symbolic of the family's forebearers and the bounty of the harvest, ceremoniously carried inside the house on Christmas Eve and placed in the corner under the icons. The didukh remained in the house until the eve of the Epiphany when it was taken outside on the yard and burned.

krashanka (pl. krashanky): A solid-coloured Easter egg (usually red); a part of the blessed Easter foods.

Kupalo: An ancient Slavic holiday in celebration of the summer solstice (June 24).

lira: Lyre, a type of musical instrument.

namitka: A type of head covering worn by Ukrainian women. It was made from a piece of flaxen linen, approximately a half metre wide and up to five metres long, and tied about the head in various ways. The ends of the namitka were sometimes decorated with embroidered designs. In Hutsulshchyna, Bukovyna and regions of Lviv and Stanyslaviv it was called peremitka and rantukh.

panakhyda: Prayers for the dead.

parastas: Church service for the dead.

paska: A rich, round Easter bread, up to a half metre in size in some regions, decorated with elaborate dough ornaments with the cross typically forming the central motif.

peremitka: See entry under namitka.

posydinnia: Ritual sitting with the body of the deceased inside the house before the funeral and burial.

Pylypivka: Advent; a 39-day period before Christmas observed as a season of solemn preparation for the Nativity. The Advent period begins on the Sunday nearest to St. Andrew's Day (November 30) and lasts until Christmas Eve.

pyrohy: Boiled or baked dumplings filled with potatoes, cabbage or groats.

pysanka (pl. pysanky): A decorated egg, blessed by the priest and used in various rites and rituals of the Easter season; not for eating.

saltseson: A combination of meats, usually pork, cooked, seasoned and made into a pressed loaf.

trembita: A type of musical instrument, popular among the Hutsuls.

Voznesennia: Ascension Day; celebrated on the fifth Thursday after Easter.

Yordan (also Vodokhryshchi, Bohoiavlennia): The Feast of the Epiphany (January 6). Traditionally the end of the Christmas season.

Zeleni sviata: Literally "Green Holidays"; the Ukrainian name for the Feast of the Trinity, observed on the fiftieth day after Easter. It was the first in the series of holidays of the summer cycle and marked by the decoration of the house with greenery.

Index

Toponymy of Settlements Where Photographs in this Volume were Taken*

SETTLEMENT		COUNTY	
Ukrainian Name	Polish Name	Ukrainian Name	Polish Name
Berezhnytsia Korolivska (now Berezhnytsia)	Bereźnica Królewska	Zhydachiv	Żydaczów
Bolekhiv	Bolechów	Dolyna	Dolina
Demenka Lisova	Demenka Leśna	Zhydachiv	Żydaczów
Denysiv	Denysów	Ternopil	Tarnopol
Dovhe	Dołhe	Tovmach	Tłumacz
Hnizdychiv	Hnizdyczów	Zhydachiv	Żydaczów
Humeniv	Humenów	Kalush	Kałusz
Izydorivka (now Sydorivka)	Izydorówka	Zhydachiv	Żydaczów
Kosiv	Kosów	Kosiv	Kosów
Liubsha	Lubsza	Zhydachiv	Żydaczów
Nezvyshchi	Nieźwiska	Horodenka	Horodenka
Rozhniativ	Rożniatów	Dolyna	Dolina
Strusiv	Strusów	Terebovlia	Trembowla

Tyshkivtsi	Tyszkowce	Horodenka	Horodenka
Turady	Turady	Zhydachiv	Żydaczów
Tseniava	Ceniawa	Dolyna	Dolina
Tsutsylivtsi (now Vilkhivtsi)	Cucułowce	Zhydachiv	Żydaczów
Voltsniv	Wołcniów	Zhydachiv	Żydaczów
Yaikivtsi	Jajkowce	Zhydachiv	Żydaczów
Zabolotivtsi	Zabłotowce	Zhydachiv	Żydaczów
Zarohyzno	Zarogóżno	Zhydachiv	Żydaczów
Zbora	Zbora	Kalush	Kałusz
Zhydachiv	Żydaczów	Zhydachiv	Żydaczów

* This gazetteer lists the names of the settlements and their respective counties as they were in 1900.

SETTLEMENT		COUNTY	
Ukrainian Name	Polish Name	Ukrainian Name	Polish Name
Stryhantsi	Stryhańce	Tovmach	Tłumacz